4.00

THE TORONTO BLESSING

The Toronto Blessing

What would the Holy Spirit say?

Robert J. Kuglin

HORIZON BOOKs

CAMP HILL, PENNSYLVANIA

Horizon Books
3825 Hartzdale Drive
Camp Hill, PA 17011

ISBN: 0-88965-131-0

© 1996 by Robert J. Kuglin
All rights reserved

Printed in the United States of America

96 97 98 99 00   5 4 3 2 1

Unless otherwise indicated, Scripture taken from
the NEW AMERICAN STANDARD BIBLE
© 1960, 1962, 1963, 1968, 1971, 1972, 1973, 1975, 1977, 1995
by the Lockman Foundation, La Habra, CA.
All rights reserved.

Scripture labeled "KJV" is taken from
the HOLY BIBLE, Authorized King James Version.

On the cover: Toronto, Ontario, Canada,
with the CN Tower and the Skydome in the foreground.

To my wonderful wife Gwen,
a faithful companion
with me in the gospel for forty-three years, and
who has modeled Christ to thousands

Table of Contents

Foreword

When the Board of Directors asked me as Publisher to bring out some books on current issues, and since they had made it clear they would allow some controversial subject matter, we turned toward what has become known as the "Toronto Blessing." My choice for the assignment was Bob Kuglin. I have known and respected him for years. He is no novice. Further, for years his ministry of evangelism around the world has been marked by supernatural events.

I deemed him well-qualified to investigate and analyze a major happening among evangelicals. Remember as you read, this is written by a man who understands this kind of phenomena and has walked in the midst of things like these for most of the years of his ministry. This volume is Rev. Robert Kuglin's response to the "Toronto Blessing."

K. Neill Foster, Publisher
Camp Hill, Pennsylvania
August 1996

Preface

I was just finishing a speaking tour of the People's Republic of China when I became deathly ill. The plan was for me to take my seventh extended trip to the Republic of the Philippines before returning to Canada. But after a few days in Hong Kong, it became clear that God was intervening and giving different directions for the end of 1995. In my weakened condition, Cathay Pacific Airlines graciously rearranged my flights and looked after me royally on my way home to Regina, on the Western Canadian Prairies.

What surprise did God have for me this time? I had a wonderful year of ministry in 1994 with over 11,000 people responding publicly in India and the Philippines, and 1995 was even more blessed of the Lord. Because I became the instrument through which the Holy Spirit so marvelously worked, the church in India decided to extend to me their highest honor—1,000 red roses in numerous garlands. (While it did fit their Indian culture, this staid Canadian was thoroughly embarrassed with the show of affection.)

Then I went to China where I was told that I was the first Caucasian evangelical to preach in the government-directed Three-Self Church since the expulsion of the missionaries in 1949 during the Cultural Revolution. Speaking in Watchman Nee's original Little Flock Church in Quanzhou was a very special experience. To give the elders there permission to print one million copies of my book, *I Was the Devil's Egg*, was far more than I had asked the Lord to do.

I discovered long ago that when God intervenes in what I had thought were His plans, He has a different ministry than what I envisioned.

While I was still recuperating and "watching and praying," Dr. K. Neill Foster of Horizon Books phoned to see if I would write a book on the Toronto Blessing. This caught me completely by surprise. Though I had read a lot about it, I had not been interested enough to attend even one service despite several opportunities. I had not even bothered to catalog the materials.

After a few days of prayer, my heart warmed up to the task and I began to study the renewal in earnest. If I took on this project, I wanted it to meet certain criteria:

1. While the book must be an exploration of the phenomena, it must be easy to read. Some of the other titles already in print would be read by academics, but certainly not by the general public where it was needed most.

2. It must not only explore every-

thing possible about the Toronto Blessing, but it also would have to teach. It would not be sufficient to give the cold hard facts. The readers who want direction must be able to find it.

3. I must not be guided by any of my own prejudices. I must have an open mind, even on some points of theology and practice that I had made conclusions about in bygone years.

4. I would attend as many Toronto Airport Vineyard services as I could over the course of one week. This I would do incognito, so I would not get tailored answers to my queries and observations.

5. It must be a worthwhile enough project in order to demand a number of months away from my fruitful overseas ministries. Does the church at large need the book? Will people read it? And will they listen to what I have to say? With my heart and mind giving affirmative answers to these questions, I postponed an evangelistic tour to India.

6. I would have to seek advice of godly people who were disciplined in areas in which I lacked knowledge and experience.

7. I would need to have a consistent system to show people where I received my information through careful use of

endnotes. Through over forty years of ministry, I have discovered that the general public does not refer to the notes, but academics enjoy them.

Almost everyone responded when I approached them for information and suggestions. Materials, solicited and otherwise, have come from across Canada and the United States in great volumes. People have been so gracious when I have phoned them, even at inconvenient hours.

I appreciate all those who wrote to tell me of the help received at the Toronto Blessing. There have been an equal number who sent cautions and their reasons why. If these items have not been used in the book, I beg your indulgence. If I put everything in, it would be a small library. My goal has been to make the book short enough to be read and long enough to be worth reading.

My wife, Gwen, has been a faithful critic of each paragraph. Her patience has shone brightly through an exhausting and upset schedule. She continues as manager of our city's largest Christian bookstore, as a tutor for some student wives and in music at our local church. I felt I could not ask her to do anything more, but she volunteered.

The poetry of one of my favorite writers seemed to fit nearly everything I wanted to say. So I have borrowed from the repertoire of the late Dr. A.B. Simpson, giving just one stanza of a hymn to finalize each chapter. I have prayed the following words many times. I trust the reader will do the same.

> Search me, O God, search me and know
>   my heart;
> Try me and prove me in the hidden part;
> Cleanse me and make me holy, as Thou
>   art,
> And lead me in the way everlasting.
>
> Thou art the same today and yesterday:
> Oh, make Thy life in me the same alway.
> Take from my heart the things that
>   pass away;
> Lead, lead me in the way everlasting.[1]

Endnotes

1. A.B. Simpson, "Search Me, O God," *Hymns of the Christian Life* (Camp Hill, PA: Christian Publications, 1978), #239.

Chapter 1

Foundation for Revival

The year was 1974. I was traveling from revival/evangelistic meetings in Lock Haven, Pennsylvania to Rome, New York. This would be my last crusade before returning to our country home 100 miles northwest of Toronto, Canada.

I knew the greatest revivalist of the previous century, evangelist Charles Grandison Finney, had enjoyed a tremendous revival in Rome, New York. Now I was trusting God for another great moving of the Holy Spirit in an area that had once again become very needy.

To prepare my heart further for the Rome meetings, I read Finney's *Lectures on Revival* as I traveled.[1] Generally speaking, I liked what I read except for one thing which bothered me. I jotted into my notes: "Revivals are worked up, not prayed down." I put a question mark after my statement.

As I sat in a bus depot reading and awaiting a bus transfer, the thought came to me again in a later chapter of the book. How could the editors allow the same idea to slip through twice? Finney must have intended it to be so. What did he actually mean? It prompted me to rethink what I was doing.

I soon discovered that, in reality, I believed the same way Finney did on the subject of revival. Fervent prayer certainly is necessary, but it is not the secret nor the foundation. Prayer is a solid part of the structure, but it is not the bottom line.

Upon arriving in Rome, I was taken by the host pastor to my temporary apartment, not far from the church. After getting settled, I looked out my bedroom window. Across a small park, I saw the large cathedral-like church that had been built for those who had responded to Finney's ministry. Though his meetings started in a house on December 25, 1825, during those three weeks of ministry there were more than 500 converts who needed a place for worship and discipleship training.[2] This was a remarkable work of God, considering that Rome had only a few thousand people at the time.

During the course of my own ministry in that city, I did see a limited working of the Holy Spirit. A few people accepted Christ as Savior, others professed healing and a few sought to be filled with the Holy Spirit. But it came far short of what I had seen in other places, such as Tampa and Orlando, Florida. What was wrong? Had God changed in the span of a few months?

The meetings in Florida had taken me from my Canadian pastorate near Toronto to full-time itinerant ministry on the basis of Ephesians 4:11-13:

> And He gave some as apostles, and some as prophets, and some as evangelists, and some as pastors and teachers, for the equipping of the saints for the work of service, to the building up of the body of Christ; until we all attain to the unity of the faith, and of the knowledge of the Son of God, to a mature man, to the measure of the stature which belongs to the fulness of Christ.

I had concluded that the work of the evangelist was in the same realm of ministry as that of the pastor-teacher. It was merely a stepped-up or more intense ministry to build up the body of Christ both in quantity and quality, both physically and spiritually. And God was honoring His Word.

I have always been hard on myself. After I became a Christian in 1948, this took on a different form. I soon realized that Jesus took my sin and forgave me, even though He had not been involved in my wrongdoing. In order to be Christlike, I needed to be willing to accept responsibility when things went badly by earthly standards, even when I thought I was innocent in a particular situation.

This mind-set led me to examine my heart.

3

Had I neglected an area in my life? Was God now displeased? I was no longer "keeping short accounts" with Him, as I had been taught. I was now "keeping *current* accounts," which I found to be much more effective. Why wait until the end of the day to discuss the temperature of my spiritual walk with God?

I also discovered early in my ministry that I could spot problems very quickly, but at first that was all I saw. I further learned that a person with a critical *spirit* or heart could not see beyond the problems, but a person with a critical *mind* and a mellow heart could both see the problems and come up with the solutions.

As I was wrestling through these issues, an elder whom I took to be single asked to take me to dinner. It was the first Friday night of the Rome meetings. In a rustic restaurant he told me that the pepper steak was delicious and the best buy. Noting his obesity and the stains on his completely out-of-fashion tie, I observed that he may have fit Paul's description of the Cretans in Titus 1:12.

I also observed that according to First Timothy 2:2-7 he did not appear to qualify for eldership. First, he did not have a wife. Second, he therefore would not have children in subjection. And third, he was not temperate. In time, I learned that some of my observations were wrong.

"Thank you, but no," I said. "Eating green peppers just before I speak is not a good idea. I think I'll have the minced steak instead." I noticed it was the same price and assumed that economy was what he had in mind.

When the waitress came to take our orders, he said, "Two pepper steaks."

Instead of arguing, I decided it was the better part of valor to eat what was set before me for conscience' sake and not ask any questions, as admonished in First Corinthians 10:25. I also prayed that the Lord would sanctify the food and that I would not be too bilious when it came time for me to speak.

During the meal I discovered that my new friend was indeed married. His wife lived only a few miles away. I listened intently to his version of the separation. In my heart I tried to heed Proverbs 18:13, which advocates hearing all sides of an event before coming to a conclusion.

His face became drawn as he talked. His voice rose as he mentioned her name. He was attracting attention to our table on a subject that I thought unwise to discuss loudly in a public place. He was a very bitter man, looking for a peace, joy and happiness that eluded him.

To change the topic, I turned his attention to Charles Finney, the big church building and the revival of 1825-1826. The elder exclaimed, "I am praying that God will do it again. Do it again! Do it again!!"

"He can. And He will if we will meet the conditions," I responded. "It starts with us. Let us pay for our meal, but leave it with a sizable tip for the kind waitress. Then let us immediately go to see your wife. The meeting can wait for us. You will apologize to her. You will go the extra mile and tell her you are taking all the blame, just like Jes—"

He jumped to his feet, yelling out, "Never! Never! Never!"

If I had been embarrassed before, it had nothing on this.

All eyes in the restaurant were on us as I said to him, "Then God will *not* do it again! The leadership must humble themselves in order for the Holy Spirit to work in revival refreshing."

We ate our pepper steak in silence and then went to the church.

Again a few people responded to the altar call. The pastor requested the elders to help in the counseling and praying. My dinner host for the evening came to assist, of course. So I went to him as he piously knelt beside a seeker, put my hand on his shoulder and said, "Never. Never. Never." And I directed him back to his pew. I was never accustomed to "playing church"; if we can't do it the way God said in His Word, then why bother doing it at all? I was tired of seeing so much "wood, hay, straw" (1 Corinthians 3:12-14).

Finney preached and practiced Second Chronicles 7:14, and so do I:

> [If] My people who are called by My name *humble themselves* and pray, and seek My face and turn from their wicked ways, then I will hear from

heaven, will forgive their sin, and will heal their land. (italics mine).

In true revival or renewal, humbling oneself is always foundational. There must be prayer. We must seek God's face. We must turn from our wicked ways. But these last three are ineffectual without the first. God's people must humble themselves before prayer can be answered and before the last two points can be effectively produced. Only then will God hear from heaven, forgive our sin and heal our land.

This is what Finney preached. And this is what he meant when he said that revivals are not prayed down, they are worked up. Yes, there is the God-ward side to revival. But there is also the human part. And with very rare exceptions, the human part comes first when God sovereignly moves in revival power.

As we examine in detail "The Laughing Revival," now being called "The Toronto Blessing," keep in mind Second Chronicles 7:14. Read it again and again. Memorize it. Meditate upon it. The Word of God will keep us in proper perspective as we deal with the pros and cons of the phenomena of both past and present.

Let us ask searching questions: What would the Holy Spirit say about present occurrences in Toronto and numerous other locations? Does He smile with approval on the Toronto Airport Christian Fellowship (formerly the Toronto Airport Vineyard Christian Fellowship)? Is this something to be avoided? Or could there possibly be a middle road between the two? Is the Holy Spirit grieved by our ignorance?

It is imperative that we understand that revival is initiated by humbling ourselves. Humbling ourselves will not necessarily bring revival (except to ourselves), but all methods and preparations fall far short of the revival goal without the humbling. This is key!

> O fire of God, begin in me;
>> Burn out the dross of self and sin,
> Burn off my fetters, set me free,
>> And make my heart a heaven within.[3]

Endnotes

1. Charles G. Finney, *Lectures on Revival* (Minneapolis, MN: Bethany, 1988).

2. Garth M. Rosell and Richard Dupuis, eds., *The Memoirs of Charles G. Finney: The Complete Restored Text* (Grand Rapids, MI: Zondervan, 1989), p. 157.

3. A.B. Simpson, "Burn On!" *Hymns of the Christian Life* (Camp Hill, PA: Christian Publications, 1978), #246.

Chapter 2

Preparation for the Toronto Blessing

"Wow!" was my first impression upon entering the Toronto Airport Christian Fellowship building. The place was enormous. *They certainly have provided a big enough place for the Holy Spirit to do something,* I thought.

My mind flashed back to my early days of ministry on the east coast of Canada. We had a dingy little clapboard building that seated a mere ninety people. It became a frustration to me. Nobody seemed to want anything bigger or better. I would hold special meetings in larger rented quarters, but we always had to come back to "The Mission."

On one of my district superintendent's many visits, he asked me to take him on a tour of the city's church buildings. I was delighted to do so. Our city was one of the oldest in Canada and had great historic interest with some architecturally alluring structures.

After seeing a number of them—First United, Immanuel Baptist, the Presbyterian and others—Dr. Bailey requested that I drive to the one where I preached. When I started to get out of the car, he asked that we just remain and look. After a long silence, he said, "Bob, you say that you have faith."

I nodded.

"Then why are you pastoring such a small flock that still meets in a hovel?" he queried.

That spurred me on. I was determined to do better. We laid plans for a much larger building with full-blown strategies on how to fill it for Jesus and for the sake of lost souls.

One summer I had an evangelist come for the last two weeks of July. Some churches closed for the summer so we were able to rent the largest church building in the city. It was just what we wanted. It could be used for small crowds, and big ones could be accommodated with its unique expansion walls. The meetings were extended into the second week of August. We saw over 150 first-time decisions for Christ.

But I had a very severe problem. My overseers would not allow me to build a church for more than 120 people. I could break away from the denomination and become independent and do my thing. Or I could adhere to Hebrews 13:17:

> Obey your leaders, and submit to them; for they keep watch over your souls, as those who will give an account. Let them do this with joy and not with

grief, for this would be unprofitable for you.

I chose to stick with God's Word, not knowing that some day because of obedience the Lord of the Harvest would give me a far greater ministry than I ever could have had in any one city. However, as a pastor I never had a building big enough to really handle a full revival. This could not be said of the Toronto Airport Christian Fellowship (TACF). I counted the chairs. There were 1,964 on a Sunday morning, although they had originally started in a building that seated only 360.

In the TACF building there were professionally made banners—very large ones, longer than many churches are wide—in English, French, German and Chinese: "That we may walk in God's love and give it away." If I were doing it, I would have put up Bible texts, because it is the Word that quickens. But at least they had prepared, quite unlike some pastors who seemingly pray, "Lord, bless my lack of preparation."

Directly in the center at the front, there was a large, high platform on which the "worship team" performed. (Music plays such an important part in almost all religions that I will devote a later chapter to it.) In front of this music platform there was a much smaller, lower one for the speaker. This bothered me. Music and singing seemed to be much more important than the reading and preaching of God's Word. The Bible was not given a prominent place.

There were also "stop signs" telling people to keep off the platform. One would think that this would not be necessary. However, when the Kuglin Family traveled across North America in evangelistic meetings, we found it was. Many times we had to protect our musical instruments from people who felt it necessary to run their fingernails across the delicate keys of our vibraphone, blow into a trombone or strum a guitar. So my sympathies were with TACF rather than with those who might criticize the "stop signs."

Included in the church complex is a sizable bookstore. Most of the titles were of an extreme charismatic nature. There were very few books that would be found in a major evangelical bookstore. But at least they were providing books. And did not Paul exhort Timothy to "give attention to the public reading of Scripture, to exhortation and teaching" (1 Timothy 4:13)? Let any who criticize the titles sold at TACF provide better reading material at a price the average Christian can afford.

I arrived early enough to get a good seat and found a spot where I could properly observe every part of the service. A welcome feature was a cafeteria for those like myself who had traveled many miles to get there. Leaving my coat draped over the back of the seat to hold it, I went to the cafeteria for a snack.

Washroom facilities, however, were not adequate for the expected crowds. When meetings and after-meetings go on for hours, this can be a big problem.

During my research, I picked up information folders in hotels and motels around Toronto. A typical brochure revealed an overall pattern. Under "Houses of Worship" were listed Anglican, Mosque, Presbyterian, Roman Catholic, Synagogue, Ukrainian Catholic, United Church of Canada and Toronto Airport Christian Fellowship. All had their addresses and phone numbers—some even had fax numbers!

Even the casual reader will notice that there are some denominations sadly missing in this free advertising, some of whom have large churches in the area. The evangelical church should take advantage of these respectable methods. The Toronto Airport Christian Fellowship certainly is.

For TACF conventions, the hotels and motels around the Toronto Pierson Airport offer special discounts on both rooms and food.[1] Anybody showing proof of registration or attendance qualifies. There are also discounts offered by some airlines for those flying to Toronto to attend the meetings. These things are not done in some mystical way by the Holy Spirit. There was well-planned organization here.

The leaders of the Toronto Blessing are also employing modern technology. They use cordless mikes. Large screens are arranged so everybody can see the center of activity by remote screening. They are also on the Internet.

Well-planned organization will not bring about revival. But without some very good planning, we cannot properly expect that God will do much for us. He will not do for us what He expects us to do. The planning may not be specifically designed to bring about a revival. It may simply be that God sees a pastor who can be trusted with a revival because of his faithfulness and transparency. In the case we are dealing with in this book, revival appears to be a specific intention by leadership, as may be seen in the next chapter.

As I personally surveyed the facilities and witnessed the preparation, my mind went back to a pastor's prayer retreat in the city of Calgary, Alberta, Canada. At the close of one prayer session the district superintendent, Rev. Roy McIntyre, said:

> I have not been praying with you. Please forgive me. I have been analyzing your prayers. Many of you prayed for a great revival. But not one of you has a building large enough to see a revival in your community. I challenge you to go back to your people and convince them to build twice the size in anticipation of what you have prayed for.[2]

Many of those pastors took the challenge. And when revival came in 1971 and 1972,[3] The Christian and Missionary Alliance had buildings in many towns and cities across the prairies that were large enough to contain a revival for the saints and an awakening for the sinners. Other denominations were touched also, but not to the same degree, perhaps because they had not prepared in faith to handle the results. It is interesting to note that the more charismatic groups did not cooperate in that awakening, some claiming that they were seeing more happen in their regular services than others did in the revival.

Besides examining the Toronto Blessing, this book will endeavor to compare the fruit of the 1971-1972 Western Canada revival with the 1994-1995 Eastern Canadian meetings.

> Baptize with fire this soul of mine;
>   Endue me with Thy Spirit's might
> And make me by Thy power divine
>   A burning and a shining light.[4]

Endnotes

1. *Spread the Fire*, August 1995, Vol. 1, Issue 4, pp. 22f.

2. Roy McIntyre, Western Canadian District Prayer Conference, September 1965.

3. *Canadian Midwest Memo*, January 1972.

4. A.B. Simpson, "Burn On!" *Hymns of the Christian Life* (Camp Hill, PA: Christian Publications, 1978), #246.

Chapter 3

A Prophecy in Toronto

I am not adverse to happenings that are not recorded in the Bible. We all have these every day. What reader has not been in a motorized vehicle this week? There were no cars in the Bible. I *am* adverse to happenings that are anti-scriptural or practices that the Bible does not condone, either directly or by implication.

We are to "give earnest heed to the voice of the LORD [our] God, and do what is right in His sight, and give ear to His commandments, and keep all His statutes" (Exodus 15:26). There are promises throughout the Scriptures that are based on these conditions.

Every one of us is given the same Word of God:

> Go therefore and make disciples of all the nations, baptizing them in the name of the Father and the Son and the Holy Spirit, teaching them to observe all that I commanded you; and lo, I am

with you always, even to the end of the age. (Matthew 28:19-20)

All of us have this call, and we interpret it in the way we think God wants us to work for Him. To one that means to become a nurse. To another, a farmer. To yet another, a politician. To me, it first meant becoming a pastor for twenty years with an ability to solve problems and start new churches. Eventually it led to becoming an itinerant evangelist for another twenty-four years.

But how can I find out where to go and when? The Bible does not tell me. I have to make choices which I believe are directed by the Holy Spirit, who uses diverse methods. There have been times when He has used the prophetic voice of an overseer. On other occasions, He has used dreams to direct me, even caution me. Let me tell you of one.

It was very vivid, in full color. I awakened in a cold sweat and told my wife. It was just as real as if it had already happened; I could remember every detail. In my dream, I was on an Indian reservation. By invitation I arrived at a certain home where I was greeted by one of the largest women I have ever seen. Her red-dyed hair stuck out as though she had been in an explosion. She wore a man's red-, black- and white-checkered shirt that hung loose over bright blue double-knit slacks (which I assure you were *not* slack). Certain teeth were missing, the gaps vividly exposed as she laughed uncontrollably.

In my dream she gave me a large white gran-
ite mug. It was so big that I could put my whole
hand into the handle. She then disappeared
into an adjoining room and laughed and
laughed and laughed. The mug was filled with
poisoned tea!

My very next meetings were on a reservation
in northern Canada.[1] My wife interpreted the
dream by saying, "God is warning you not to go."
Obviously she loved me and did not want to be
widowed at fifty years of age.

I interpreted it differently according to my
prejudice; I wanted to go. So I replied, "This is
what God wants. He is merely telling me to be on
the alert." Things like these are difficult to interpret, if in fact God wants us to interpret them at
all.

But everything happened just as I stated above,
except that I had the minister's wife with me as
an interpreter and she was also given a mug. She
interpreted for the personal counseling sessions,
while her husband did the interpreting for the
services.

When the pastor's wife was handed her cup, I
said, "Mary [not her real name], don't drink that
stuff. I'll tell you why later." She replied that she
was not obligated to drink it since she was not
invited. But I was a guest in the house. If I refused hospitality, the whole community would
find out and nobody would come to the meetings. I immediately threw my drink out the front
door. The woman came back into the room,

looked into my cup and again laughed and laughed.

Later, after explaining my actions to Mary, she replied, "I'm so glad God warned you. That woman puts hexes on people. They really work. Thanks for warning me."

And now with an understanding of where I am coming from, I want to present the prophecy of Marc A. Dupont, a Vineyard minister. It was published under his name in a release by Mantle of Praise Ministries, Inc., and circulated by TACF in March 1994.[2] The prophecy is in two parts. The first part was prophesied by Dupont in Toronto in 1992. The second part was given in Vancouver, BC, Canada in 1993.

It is important to carefully consider these two prophecies since what has happened in Toronto is believed to be validated by them. They appear to have been the driving force behind it all. Such validation is referred to by scholars as a "prophetic theology." In order to present this material as fairly as possible, the indented portions that follow are the prophecies in the same grammatical and structural form in which they have been widely circulated, except for some minor spelling corrections. My remarks are interspersed, but are *not* indented, to avoid confusion.

PART ONE: MAY 1992, WHILE IN TORONTO FOR THE AREA OF SOUTHERN ONTARIO.

I. A vision of water falling over and onto an extremely large rock. The amount of water was similar to Niagara Falls.

A. Toronto will be the place where the much living water will be flowing with great power, even though at the present time both the church and the city are like big rocks—cold and hard against God's love and His Spirit. The waterfall shall be so powerful that it will break the big rocks up into small stones that can be used in building the kingdom. Those stones which resist the Spirit will be broken down into dust: therefore the living waters and judgment shall first come on the existing church of Toronto. There will not be any true unity among the churches until they begin to respond to the prophetic voice of the Father's voice. The breaking of pride and stiffness will result in stones, (Christians and churches), which can fit together in the master builder's hands. At this moment, the living stones are unable to fit together compactly because of major protrusions on the stones, which in effect keep the leaders at arms length from one another. These protrusions are pride and arrogance.

Notice the threat to those who resist. This is typical of many things I have read about the group and heard in the meetings. It also appears to me that the leadership in the Toronto Blessing display the pride and arrogance mentioned above. Theirs is an attitude of "you need what we have," instead of an adherence to the admonition, "Do nothing from selfishness or empty conceit, but with humility of mind let each of you regard one another as more important than himself" (Philippians 2:3).

> B. That rock shall be transformed from a rock of death into the Rock of Psalm 40 and the rock that Jesus said would prevail against the gates of hell. As the people of God in Toronto really cry out in their hearts for God, the Lord is going to respond by placing our feet on His rock of intimacy with Him. Our feet shall then be transformed into feet which can go forward with the gospel against the gates of hell. Many will hear the new song that God will [be] putting in the mouths of His people and many will come to fear the Lord. A new song will spring up from the heart of the Church as we respond to the moving of the Holy Spirit. Not so much literally a "new song," but a new freedom of worshiping with God's favor and presence resting on us. In that freedom many

churches will begin to take worship out into the public arenas. Worship and music in the public places, where the unchurched can hear them, [are] going to play a significant role in what God is going to be doing. The artists and musicians of Toronto are going to experience a strong move of God's Spirit.

There have been many churches in Toronto doing a great work for God for as long as I, who grew up in Ontario, can remember. Perhaps this was a prophecy to tell Vineyard to "get on the ball," stop the sheep-stealing and get some goats converted. During my tenure as executive director of Sermons from Science at the Canadian National Exhibition, up to 10,000 people prayed the sinner's prayer each August.

The Toronto Blessing took over two years to do less at a tremendous overall cost. Now they are sending teams into the streets to offer free prayer to anyone who comes along. But it really isn't typical praying. One member of the team puts his hand on the forehead of the person who stops. The other is the catcher. I have not personally seen this, except in photographs published in the Airport church's official paper, *Spread the Fire*. Upon investigation I discovered that the aim is to either "slay" the person or get them to laugh.

C. Like the time of Elijah many who are privately going to the "mountain" and seeking the face of the Lord are going to find that there are many others who are also deeply crying out to the Lord. It is just going to be, however, that most of those who are really interceding and crying out to God are not mainstream. Most of them are currently outside of the visible picture of what is happening right now. There will be a radical move in late '93 and through out '94 of many ordinary Christians beginning to form on their own prayer groups of intercession for the city, the nation and the peoples.

Since there was no fulfillment of this, a shadow is cast on the rest of the prophecy. Perhaps Mr. Dupont had not heard of the "Ten-Forty Window" prayer concern which was, and is, being used in a mighty way to raise up prayer warriors around the world.

To be a prophecy, the prophet must speak before the event, not after the thing prophesied has already taken place, so the "Ten-Forty Window" concept cannot be considered a fulfillment of Dupont's prophecy. Further, "on their own" speaks of spontaneity. We hear of people spending long hours "on the floor," but not praying and interceding for their city.

The "Ten-Forty Window" concept was initiated by Bill Bright, founder and president of Campus Crusade for Christ International, a man respected in Christian circles worldwide. It is the term used to describe that part of the world between the tenth and fortieth lines of latitude, north of the equator. The concept is a call for all Christians to focus prayer on this most densely populated area of the world. It contains most of China, all of India, the Near East and north and central Africa, to name a few. It is also the area most resistant to the gospel.

The significance of Dr. Bright's contribution is supported by a news item in *Alliance Life,* which stated, "Dr. William R. 'Bill' Bright, founder and president of Campus Crusade for Christ International, and one of the most vigorous Christian evangelists in the world, has won the 1996 Templeton Prize for Progress in Religion."[3]

D. The disciples of Jesus were gathered from many different areas of life. The leaders of the coming move of the Lord are also going to be coming from many different areas. Many of them are also not mainstream, but many will be without a lot of previous experience, but they will end up both being used by God in evangelism,[4] signs and wonders, and also in discipling new converts. This is not to say that brand new converts will end up as leaders, because obviously Jesus' apostles had grown up knowing teaching as children, and had been personally discipled by Jesus for three years or more. But it does mean that many current leaders will not be in leadership of what is to come, because many current leaders will disqualify themselves by not responding to what the Father will be saying. As Jesus said "to those that have more shall be given, and to those who do not have even what they have will be taken away"!

E. Like Jerusalem, Toronto will end up being a sending out place. It is of God that there are so many internationals in this area. The Lord is going to be sending out many people, filled with His Spirit with strong gifting, vision and love to the nations on all continents. There are going to be new Bible schools, training centers and leadership schools raised up in the move that is coming. These schools will have a focus not only on Bible knowledge, but also on training in healing broken hearts and setting the captives free (training means actually doing by learning rather than just studying from textbooks) and on developing intimacy with the Father.

Anybody who has studied church history will know that Antioch in Syria was the center of Christian activity and the center of early Christian missions, not Jerusalem. Look it up in any Bible dictionary.[5] And anybody who knows Canadian church history knows of numerous such training centers as Mr. Dupont says are "going" to happen. In my province I know of at least twelve, and we have a population of only one million.

This is more like emotional preaching rather than prophecy. Note the use of Dupont's phrase, "I believe," rather than "thus saith the Lord," in the next phase of his prophecy:

> II. As God's rock began to be raised up out of the stony city it began to be shaped like a huge dam, which to some degree stored [up] the living water. But at the same time the water began to be poured out of the dam and began to flow west quite strongly.

> A. I saw those waters like a strong raging river head west all the way to the Rocky Mountains, and then go north along the eastern edge of the mountains and then go east again across the plains. In essence there was like a huge circle of water that wrapped around the plains of Canada. As the waters originating from Toronto began to go into the plains areas they began to find wells or pockets of water in many areas of the plains. I believe these wells are symbolic of remnant areas of Mennonites

and other groups that experienced revival years and years ago, but like deep unused wells have not been tapped into for a long time. As these waters began to mix the wells came to life and began to become like geysers shooting water up for hundreds of feet. People began to flock to many areas of the plains, and these areas became centers of revival which then spread to other cities and towns. I believe that there is a strong contingent of prayer warriors, who are descendants of people many years ago (possibly a hundred years ago, app.) who have continued to seek the face of God for their country.

Perhaps Mr. Dupont has not read of the prairie revivals, the latest in 1971 and 1972, on which I will comment later. There has been a concerted effort to spread the "Laughing Revival" to the prairies. At the time of this writing, it has been pretty much a failure, with many curious people, but little to show for the effort at the end of rallies. Talk of participating churches "bursting at the seams" is simply a figment of somebody's keen imagination.

Mr. Dupont should also remember that many places on the prairies are less than 100 years old. My city of Regina, for example, reached its ninetieth birthday as a community, not just as a city, in 1996. No wonder he used the very indefinite wording. Prophecy is listed as a gift of the Holy Spirit in a number of places in the Bible, so the true prophet should be speaking as God moves upon him. It does appear that full truth has not emanated from the lips of this "prophet." And the reader must remember that the total Toronto Blessing is believed to be validated by this prophecy. Some of these predictions are so vague that they could mean virtually anything. Only the first one is specific, and it did not come to pass.

I have referred briefly to a previous ministry at the Canadian National Exhibition in Toronto. It was strictly a soul-saving station. The team showed fifteen Moody Institute of Science films each day. It was an extremely busy time. Counseling and follow-up had to be taken care of after Labor Day weekend.

One day one of the volunteer workers came declaring that half of California would fall into the Pacific Ocean on September 13, 1968. The team couldn't get him off the subject. He was upsetting other workers. He was not doing his job—namely, directing the many respondees to repent and receive Christ. He had to be sent home. He had been a faithful worker in his local church and at our pavilion. But when September 13 came and went, and nothing happened, he lost his ministry.

The Bible is quite explicit in Deuteronomy 18:21-22:

And you may say in you heart, "How shall we know the word which the LORD has not spoken?" When a prophet speaks in the name of the LORD, if the thing does not come about or come true, that is the thing which the LORD has not spoken. The prophet has spoken it presumptuously; you shall not be afraid of him.

If a prophet makes a prophecy and it does not come to pass, we are not to listen to him. That is an interesting ending to that chapter in the Word of God, because Dupont's "prophecy" does contain some judgments or threats. Some people have been intimidated because of Dupont's predictions of judgments upon those who would not cooperate. This Scripture assures us that we should "not be afraid of him."

I have noticed that when people get caught up in the "prophecy fad," they are very difficult to persuade that there are problems even when they are proven to be wrong. It seems that the TACF has not learned its lesson, although cautioned by some.

Joan Breckenridge of the *Toronto Globe and Mail* reports:

Many of Canada's Evangelical and Pentecostal churches say they are extremely concerned about the potential for the practice [of prophecy] getting out of control and hurting those it is meant to help.

"I have great fears about this because there is generally little accountability as to what a person says to another," said Brian Stiller, president of Evangelical Fellowship of Canada. "It simply is not controllable when you give everybody the right to say what they feel about someone else."[6]

Breckenridge is reporting on the special prophetic conference for children. Near the end of this half-page report in one of the largest papers in Canada, she writes:

At the children's service, there was no presentation of Bible stories. In an interview last week, Mr. Dupley said his goal is to ensure that the children "experience the real thing so they won't grow up being vaccinated with the Gospel."

After the service, he said that when children receive a word or vision from God, it not only builds them up in faith, "it breaks down all that religious garbage."[7]

These were children from age four to twelve from as far away as Australia. "They tumbled backward into the waiting hands of the ministry team members, who laid them out on the floor. Some rested quietly; others convulsed and moaned.[8]

Bill Dupley, who was in charge of the children's portion of the renewal service, prayed over the children, "God bless these children and release your pictures." He then called the children to come forward and tell what they had seen. An eleven-year-old said, "I saw a lion, and I'm thinking, 'Cool. It's a lion. It's God.' "[9]

If the curious did not have questions about the dangers of uncontrolled prophecy being substituted for scriptural teaching before, they certainly should after reading these reports and my reflections on the Dupont predictions.

> Take my poor heart and only let me love
>   The things that always shall abiding
>   prove.
> Bind all my heart-strings to the world
>   above,
>   And lead me in the way everlasting.
>
> Oh, let my work abide the testing day
>   That shall consume the stubble and
>   the hay;
> Oh, build my house upon the Rock I
>   pray—
>   And lead me in the way everlasting.[10]

Endnotes

1. This happened in 1981. The details of location are withheld to protect the privacy of those involved.

2. Marc Dupont, Mantle of Praise Ministries, Toronto, May 1992 and July 1993.

3. *Alliance Life,* Religious News Digest, April 10, 1996.

4. The opposite has happened; more about this in chapter 4.

5. For a couple of examples, see the following: *The International Bible Encyclopedia,* Vol. 1, n.d., p. 157; E.M. Blaiklock, *The Acts of the Apostles,* Tyndale New Testament Commentary (Grand Rapids, MI: Eerdmans, 1979), pp. 101-102.

6. Joan Breckenridge, "Church Has Faith in Prophecy," *Toronto Globe and Mail*, May 30, 1996, p. 5.

7. Ibid.

8. Ibid.

9. Ibid.

10. A.B. Simpson, "Search Me, O God," *Hymns of the Christian Life* (Camp Hill, PA: Christian Publications, 1978), #239.

Chapter 4

A Prophecy from Vancouver

Fourteen months after the initial prophecy, Marc Dupont updated it while ministering on the Canadian West Coast. This is not out of keeping with Scripture. Some of the Old Testament prophets prophesied over a period of years. As in the last chapter, the prophecies are presented in full—unedited, except for minor spelling corrections—as indented text, with my comments *not* indented, to avoid confusion. It does not make for good reading, but it does make for good understanding.

PART TWO: UPDATE JULY 5, 1993, WHILE IN VANCOUVER, CANADA. A SENSE OF URGENCY CAME ON ME FROM THE LORD, I BELIEVE WITH SOME MORE SPECIFICS FOR PRESENT LEADERSHIP OF THE BODY OF CHRIST IN TORONTO.

III. I believe the Lord indicated that the increase in evangelism, the moving of the Holy Spirit, and the call to the Christians from the Spirit for prayer [are] going to happen even this summer and autumn, with the pace accelerating into the new year. At the same time, the refiner's fire, is going to increase on leadership. As it says in Malachi 3, "who can stand" when the refiner's fire comes. Many leaders are going to be greatly shaken; they will basically go in two directions: one, more into a mode of prayer, waiting and listening to the Father, and acting out of obedience, or two, many will fall into temptation and sin, and will leave the ministry or bring judgment on themselves and their churches, which in turn will be greatly shaken. Many to the point of falling apart. For those that begin to catch what the Spirit is saying to them, they are going to be making radical steps that are going to be extremely radical for those in the churches who are not hearing what the Spirit is saying.

Just the opposite has happened regarding evangelism. The TACF has almost completely stopped evangelism. Rev. John Arnott is quoted by a number of sources as saying God called him during 1994 and 1995 to minister love to Christians instead of salvation to the lost.[1] Others obviously did the same. It may not be wrong to do what Arnott is doing—it is simply another proof that the prophecy is false. Furthermore, some other things are beginning to show. To my knowledge, the only pastors who have left the ministry have not been those who "resisted the Spirit" during the Toronto Blessing time, but rather the ones who fully entered into the phenomena.

Also, while a great wave of prayer was predicted, the opposite has taken place. In chapter 16 I have included some sayings that have grown out of the Toronto experience, such as, "Don't pray. Laugh." and "Joy! Joy! Joy! Don't pray!"[2]

> A. I also sensed from the Lord an extreme sense of danger for leaders who continue to fight the Holy Spirit. I believe that it is vital at this point, for the church leadership to be in humble prayer, for other leaders throughout Toronto.

I would add a very hearty "Amen!" But this could hardly be called a prophecy, unless Mr. Dupont is crying out for judgment upon the land.

> IV. There are going to be two basic stages in this process, which are represented by the two stages in Ezekiel's vision of the valley of dry bones.

> A. The first stage of the dry bones receiving muscle, sinew and flesh. This is the prophetic stage, where the church

and the leaders of the stage begin to seek the Father and cry out to Him for grace, mercy and a sovereign move of His Spirit. It is during this stage that leaders are going to come together for prayer, with a new attitude of humility as they realize that the Lord is calling us to do things which are completely beyond our abilities or past experiences. It is important to realize that when the Lord asked Ezekiel if the dry bones could come back to life, that Ezekiel was not completely sure, he merely responded that the Lord knew. In the same way the Father is going to be speaking things to leaders that will appear as impossible in our understanding of what can happen in our time and culture.

Rather than Ezekiel having doubt, many commentators say that "Thou knowest" refers to his faith as in, "Lord, I know *You* can." Then he goes ahead and does the very thing God told him to do. He trusted God.[3] No gimmicks! In any real revival that I have read about or witnessed firsthand, there has been the proper exposition of God's Word. No gimmicks!

B. The second stage is the apostolic stage of power and authority coming on the Church in the Toronto area. There is going to be a move of the Spirit of God on the city that is going to include powerful signs and wonders, such as in the early days of the church in Jerusalem. But also there are going to be leaders raised up in the body of Christ that are going to move in authority that will be transdenominational. These will end up being pastors of pastors [and] will be recognized as spokesmen and leaders for the government of God in the body of Christ across the denominational board. It will only be when all of the five fold offices of Ephesians are in operation, and when church leaders are coming into unity in the Spirit of the Lord that there will be a powerful release of the gospel through the church to touch cultures of S. Ontario. There will also be an increase in powerful healings and miracles.

Dupont is not clear on what he calls "the church." Is it the Airport Church or the Church at large? Prophecies need to be specific.

Instead of the unity of the Spirit as predicted, there has been further division. In December 1995, the Association of Vineyard Churches removed the Toronto Airport Christian Fellowship from its membership.[4] It is the most glaring example of the prophecy being wrong. Not only did this not happen, but the opposite occurred!

Author James A. Beverly states:

> Those experiencing the Toronto Bless-
> ing have taken "radical steps" that have
> indeed created "extreme" difficulty for
> people in other churches. That these
> steps involve uncontrollable laughter,
> shaking, roaring, barking and other
> manifestations is not specified in the
> prophecy.[5]

In *Christian Week,* June 18, 1996, Beverly further indicates that the fruit of the experience is
not uniformly positive—those "touched" by the
Blessing have sometimes provoked mean-spirited
church splits.[6]

As for healings and miracles, I'm not sure how
you can judge "powerful" ones from ones that are
not powerful. When we add to what the Scriptures say, we do come up with some odd sayings—as we will in see chapter 16.

> V. What God is going to do in S. On-
> tario and Canada will be something to-
> tally unique and special. When the
> winds of the Spirit begin to blow there
> will be elements from all four corners of
> the earth as to what is currently hap-
> pening with the body of Christ today,
> but the makeup of what will happen
> will not be like revival that has hap-
> pened anywhere else in the world. I be-

lieve that Toronto will be affected by what is currently happening in Asia, S. America, the Soviet countries, Britain and Europe, but it will still be highly unique. Some of those ingredients are going to be

1. A radical use by the Holy Spirit of artists, musicians and the performing arts. I believe that the artists and musicians are going to be essential to much of the moving of the gospel in the public areas.

The use of artists, musicians and the performing arts cannot be considered "radical." Churches have been implementing these talents for many years. And again the "prophet" uses the indefinite "I believe."

2. Church unity is going to be a growing and powerful vehicle for carrying forward the love of Christ to the city. There is going to be a new standard of cooperation among different pastors for doing outreach together and prayer together.

According to what I have already observed above, TACF erred when Arnott failed to meet the requirements which would have enabled the church to remain with the Association of Vineyard Churches. This caused another denominational

41

split instead of promoting church unity. While it is true that some pastors have attended the TACF, they have for the most part been there as spectators and not participants (see chapter 17).

> 3. I believe that there is going to be a very strong freedom for miracles, healings and signs and wonders happening very consistently in the body of Christ especially touching non-believers.

This is strong emotional preaching that encourages faith in the hearer, but should not be considered prophecy.

If we merely see non-believers healed and then allow them to go to hell, thinking all the while that they are God's children, this is a terrible thing!

> 4. The move of God in Toronto is going to be very mixed with different cultures and ethnic groups: Asian, Black, Caucasian, etc.

How else? Toronto "ranks as a leading Canadian cultural center."[7]

> 5. Many traditional denominational pastors and churches are going to be in the forefront of the move of the Spirit that will take place. I believe that many evangelical pastors are going to have a

tremendous prophetic anointing on their ministries and become spokesmen to other pastors for what the Lord is doing.

This is the end of the long prophecy as given by Marc A. Dupont. This last point is a real encouragement for pastors to begin making prophecies. Mr. Dupont really has stopped prophesying in some of his points and is merely preaching. When he says, "I believe," he certainly is not saying, "Thus saith the Lord."

In forty-four years of ministry I have seen many people, both clergy and laity, lose what had been good ministries by presuming to have the prophetic gift. Without control and the confirmation of the church, they overstepped the bounds of Scripture, "prophesied" some things that did not happen and lost the respect of the people.

During a Sunday evening service in Birmingham, Alabama in October 1973, the senior pastor gave a "prophetic utterance" that Kissinger would become the next president of the United States. (Many others in those years had prophesied that he was the antichrist.) We were starting the third week of what had the possibilities of being a full-scale revival. When he made the statement, I almost stood up to correct him, but decided to do it privately.

The following morning I suggested to him that only people with United States citizenship, who were born in the U.S., could become president.

Mr. Kissinger was born in Furth, Germany in 1923, and his family immigrated to the U.S. in 1938 to escape Hitler's persecution of the Jews.[8] He therefore could never become president.

The pastor then stated that they would change the constitution to make it possible. I said that this would be highly improbable. Although Richard Nixon, a Republican, was president, both houses were controlled by the Democrats. For Democrats to change the constitution so that a very popular Republican could become president was not likely. He retorted that I, being a Canadian, shouldn't know so much about American politics.

The meetings began to lose momentum. The board asked the pastor to retire and offered to continue his salary as long as necessary. He refused. What had been a very successful ministry almost brought a church to destruction. False prophecy did it.

Evidently Mr. Dupont has made some false prophecies. But instead of being disciplined by the Association of Vineyard Churches, he was added to the multiple staff at the Toronto Airport Vineyard Church in 1992.[9]

To summarize these last two chapters, I want to borrow from the thinking of James A. Beverley. The bottom line is this:

> [F]ifteen of the eighteen prophecies [given by Mr. Dupont] are either general, vague, or have yet to be fulfilled.

This is not a great track record on which to build certainty. While the future may bring successful closure to some of the prophecies, Christians should suspend judgment of it as a true word from the Lord.[10]

It would appear that the greater part of the Toronto Blessing was built upon these prophecies and not upon the Bible, as Paul warned in Second Timothy 4:2-4:

Preach the word; be ready in season and out of season; reprove, rebuke, exhort, with great patience and instruction. For the time will come when they will not endure sound doctrine; but wanting to have their ears tickled, they will accumulate for themselves teachers in accordance to their own desires; and will turn away their ears from the truth, and will turn aside to myths.

Gracious Heavenly Father, Hear Thy
    people's cry;
  See us! How we languish! Help us ere
    we die!
Send us by Thy Spirit Power from on
    High.
  Oh, how long we struggle! Oh, how
    hard we try!
    Helplessly we labor, Helplessly we sigh

Till Thy Spirit gives us Power from on
High.[11]

Endnotes

1. Larry Thomas, *No Laughing Matter* (Excelsior Springs, MO: Double Crown Publishing, 1995), p. 98.

2. Albert James Dager, "Special Report on Holy Laughter," *Media Spotlight*, January 1995, p. 9.

3. G. Brooks, quoted in James Compter Gray and George M. Adams, eds. *Gray and Adams Commentary,* vol. 3 (Grand Rapids, MI: Zondervan, n.d.), p. 637.

4. Doug Koop, "Toronto Airport Vineyard Released to Fly Solo," *Christian Week*, January 2, 1996, pp. 1, 5.

5. James A. Beverly, *Holy Laughter and the Toronto Blessing* (Grand Rapids, MI: Zondervan, 1995), p. 142.

6. Glen G. Scorgie, "Blessing Debated," *Christian Week,* June 18, 1996, p. 14.

7. Robert F. Nielson, *The World Book Encyclopedia*, vol. 19 (Chicago: Field Enterprises Educational Corporation, 1973), p. 262.

8. David S. Broder, *The World Book Encyclopedia*, vol. 11 (Chicago: Field Enterprises Educational Corporation, 1973), p. 260.

9. Guy Chevreau, *Catch the Fire* (Toronto: Harper-Collins, 1994), p. 28.

10. Beverley, p. 142.

11. A.B. Simpson, "Power from on High," *Hymns of the Christian Life* (Camp Hill, PA: Christian Publications, 1978), #249.

Chapter 5

Vineyard Music

The phone rang. It was Monday morning.

"Bob, wasn't the singing terrible yesterday? No hymns. Just those little ditty choruses that don't mean anything."

"But we did sing hymns," I replied. "We sang three in the first half of the service and one for closing."

"Bob, we never even opened the hymnbooks."

"I know that. They were all on the overhead. But they were hymns. And when overheads have to be picked well in advance of the service, I think there might be more preparation. I have seen pastors thumb through the hymnbook looking for hymns while the congregation is singing. He may think he is 'being led,' but he is really bluffing it."

My friend continued, "Well, yes, maybe. But then there were those little ditty choruses that don't mean a thing."

"Little ditty choruses!" I exclaimed. "Those were psalms! We sang directly from the Bible, except that the words were not wrapped in a black cover."

It was quite unlike when I was saved nearly fifty years ago. Back then we sang some pithy little things like "Climb, climb up sunshine mountain, heavenly breezes blow. Climb, climb up sunshine mountain, faces all aglow." I asked people what these little choruses meant, but I can't recall a satisfactory answer.

I am sure my friend, also in his elder years, had a similar background, but here he was downgrading the singing in our church. Why? Only one reason—he knew some of our worship singing was prepared by Vineyard. That is not fair. We need to give credit where credit is due. Vineyard musicians have been used of God to help restore the singing of God's Word through the psalms and the singing of theology from other parts of Scripture.

A good example is Brian Doerksen's chorus, "Faithful One,"[1] which we sing in our church regularly. His song is obviously based upon the Psalms where the psalmist tells of the immutable, eternal and dependable God, whom we can experience as the Deliverer in times of trouble and failure.

My friend and associate Dr. Eugene Rivard, professor of music at Canadian Bible College in Regina, Saskatchewan, says:

Bodies of music which arise from spiritual movements such as the Vineyard are generally comprised of many popular but short-lived songs. Only a few find continued use in the wider church. It is our responsibility to criticially sift the many for the few which best express our faith.[2]

This, of course, is not new with hymn writers. Some poets seem to be very prolific. Charles Wesley wrote over 6,000 hymns.[3] If a pastor taught his congregation one new Wesley hymn a week, it would take him over 115 years to learn them all!

The old hymns and spiritual songs were easy to remember because they had rhyme. A lot of Vineyard's gospel songs are blank verse. Blank verse set to music has never really caught on, either now or in the past.

Some time ago I attended a musical service in which we did nothing but sing on-the-spot requests. About ninety percent of those in attendance were people under thirty years of age. Every song they requested had rhyme. None were blank verse. And this was in a church accustomed to singing blank verse via the overhead method.

Because music has been a major element in the Toronto Blessing, it is important to examine the Vineyard approach to music. The following information is taken directly from the notes of John Wimber's *Worship Experience*, used as a textbook at a music conference held in Edmonton, Alberta and directed by Gary Best. He begins by saying the whole idea behind the concept is for us to "focus on God."[4] Who has perfect knowledge of our Creator-Redeemer? What if our concept of God is faulty? The Scriptures admonish us, rather, to meditate on the Word:

> How blessed is the man who does not walk in the counsel of the wicked, nor stand in the path of sinners, nor sit in the seat of scoffers! But his delight is in *the law of the* LORD. *And in His law he meditates day and night.* (Psalm 1:1-2, italics mine)

"Focusing on God" can indeed be dangerous. First of all, it goes against the admonition of Scripture. Second, if our concept of God is faulty, we will be focusing on a faulty God. The Scriptures, not our minds, give us the clear picture of the Lord. Let me give you a very graphic illustration from personal experience.

In September of 1974, I was invited to Columbus, Ohio to minister. The very first Sunday morning, a twenty-year-old man I shall call "Scotty" received a twelve-year, perfect-attendance pin. For most presentations of this nature, churches allow four absences a year. Scotty had not missed even one Sunday in twelve years.

When I gave the first altar call, Scotty responded. I always assist at the altar when needed and wanted, so I went to pray with Scotty. He was rigid in a squatting position with his hands palm to palm, tight against his chest. I quickly spotted the position. I don't suppose it matters, but squatting is the only position the Bible does not give for prayer.

I attempted to take his hands away from his chest and was only able to do so with some difficulty. When I let go, they flipped right back up to the usual position. Scotty was in a trance. I had prayer with him and asked if he would be back to any further services. He responded, "Every one. I do not miss." Taking that cue, I requested him to let me pray for him personally after every service.

As the days passed, I began to get information about his character and actions and awaited an appropriate time to properly look after this unusual case. He had private devotions, alone in his bedroom, morning and night. His parents were not Christians, but he had been doing this from the time he was eight years old, the very time he had started to attend Sunday school.

Back then, Scotty began wondering what God was like. He prayed that he might get a picture of God. He went to Sunday school and church but did not see what he was looking for. Then in the local newspaper he saw a picture of the Maharishi Mahesh Yogi, with his long white hair and beard. A voice said to him, "This is God." He took the picture and made a simple shrine with the Maharishi photo between two candles. He had been worshiping that picture as the Light of the World for twelve years! And all the while attending an evangelical church!

Later that week, demons were cast out of Scotty. The controlling demon called itself "Religion." It was a very ugly scene. The demons were so entrenched that they tried to kill the young man as they left. Scotty had "focused on God" for twelve years, but his concept of God was completely faulty. He focused on a false god. It is dangerous and foolish to focus on a self-made concept of God, when He is portrayed perfectly in Scripture. The only safe route is to meditate or focus on the Word of God.

Music is a powerful tool for both good and evil. I once heard an underground radio station broadcasting from Chicago which boasted that if you listened to their music from midnight to 4 a.m., you would do whatever they told you to do without knowing why.

Napoleon Bonaparte III, the infamous emperor of France from 1852 to 1870, once said, "Let me control the music of France and I care not who writes the laws. Such is the power of music."

John Wimber, writing in his *Worship Experience*, Section 15, tells us the same thing. In a service, if we follow the progressive music style he presents, "people will fall, shake, experience mass deliverances, healings, salvation, forgiveness, anointing, intercession, etc."[5]

In this he goes much too far, of course. To use the instrument of mass hysteria created by music will never bring about salvation for a lost soul.

"For by grace you have been saved through faith . . . not as a result of works" (Ephesians 2:8-9). Again, "faith comes from hearing, and hearing by the word of Christ" (Romans 10:17).

Wimber then goes on to the explain his "etc.," stating, "Prophecy is another common response."[6] Thus the implication is that if you can get the people into the right frame of mind through music, you can make them do almost anything. The reality is, however, that there are some things that can only be accomplished through God's Word. Therefore the Bible must be preached.

Wimber writes:

> It is clear why worship is subject to so much Satanic attack. His goal is to destroy our intimacy with Jesus, using every evil tactic imaginable to ruin our relationship with the King and to bring havoc in the Kingdom of God. . . . Intimacy has many counterfeits. . . . Sadly many churches today are . . . in a place [that is] dry, worked-up, empty [and] the heart of God is crushed.[7]

Again, Wimber goes too far. There is not a person or even a group of people large enough to "crush" God. The Holy Spirit can be grieved, resisted, quenched, vexed and blasphemed. But He cannot be crushed! God is all-powerful, omnipotent.

I attended a "sacred concert" as part of the 1990 Canadian Christian Booksellers Convention. One of the artists decided to sing "a song God gave me on the plane while I was returning from England. It's called 'Gloom in Heaven.' It is the result of the fall of the two Jimmys" (Jimmy Swaggert and Jim Bakker). While a songwriter may be allowed some poetic license, Scripture makes it clear that *there is no gloom in heaven*. God did not give him that song! It was likely the result of jet lag, combined with indigestion from an airplane meal.

Much of music is cultural. There is no such thing as Christian music. Music is amoral. God is not affected by it. But it is obvious that humans are, and this idea will be developed later in this chapter.

God's people sometimes say and do things that are nonscriptural, even anti-scriptural. Just as there is no gloom in heaven, it is impossible to "crush" God. He is omnipotent—all-powerful.

On page 172 of Wimber's lectures, he gets caught in his own trap. He says that many churches today are in such a place that they are "dry, worked-up, empty." He accuses the average church of having to work up intimacy with God. Then he gives an entire lecture on how Vineyard churches should do their working-up to the point of divine intimacy.

Concerning Wimber's "call to worship," he says, "The call to worship is a message to God inviting Him to visit."[8] Bless his heart. God is there all the time! The call to worship calls *us* to meet God. What he is saying comes from ideas of God such as Buddhism espouses. In Tibet, the monks blow large horns to invite their gods to awaken and visit them.[9]

It is a picture quite similar to the prophets of Baal trying to get their god to answer them in the campaign against Elijah:

> Then they took the ox which was given them and they prepared it and called on the name of Baal from morning until noon saying, "O Baal, answer us." But there was no voice and no one answered. And they leaped about the altar which they made. And it came about at noon, that Elijah mocked them and said, "Call out with a loud voice, for he is a god; either he is occupied or gone aside, or is on a journey, or perhaps he is asleep and needs to be awakened." So they cried with a loud voice and cut themselves according to their custom with swords and lances until the blood gushed out on them. And it came about when midday was past, that they raved until the time of the offering of the evening sacrifice; but there was no voice, no one answered, and no one paid attention. (1 Kings 18:26-29)

I think all Christians would agree with this

statement: "Worshiping our God properly ought to be the chief end of mankind." The emphasis here is on the word "properly." This will vary a great deal from one culture to another. We are to worship our God, in spirit and in truth. Dr. Rivard says, "No body of believers that insists upon an emotional high as the single most worshipful response to God can ever grow to maturity."[10]

After Wimber's call to worship, he then goes on to organize the service. There appears to be nothing wrong with the format. It is neutral. Dr. Rivard suggests:

> There is an inherent flaw in any worship plan which is designed to elicit a uniform response from a diverse group of believers. Outcome-oriented planning assumes that everyone has the same spiritual "instinct" and communicates with God in the same way. It smacks of manipulation. My questions are: "What happens if a person does not respond in the desired manner? Has he or she failed to worship? Do we need to tinker with the plan until it 'works'?" God communicates in diverse ways with His diverse people. He does not always choose a burning bush to attract our attention, and responses to His revelation are as varied as the people He calls to Himself.[11]

Next, Wimber asks, "How is the Lord responding? This will determine the amount of time needed to spend wooing him."[12] This is error. The Scripture plainly states, "Draw near to God and He will draw near to you" (James 4:8). Are we to woo God so He will accept us, even as a groom would woo his bride? On the contrary, the Holy Spirit woos us so we will accept Christ Jesus in all His fullness.

"Wooing God"[13] smacks of pagan worship; trying to entice God to wake up, to seduce Him is wrong. God calls us to worship. We do not call Him down to be worshiped.

After the call-to-worship songs, Wimber indicates a new "Song Selection Criteria."[14] He states, "Initially . . . songs are usually lighthearted and fun. . . . This is an introductory phase . . . 'small talk,' then less lighthearted . . . as firm contact is made with God."[15]

I took particular notice of what Dr. Wimber says about tempo. Early in the service, according to him, "tempo can be either slow or fast (but not too fast)."[16] Next he steps it up—"tempo is usually medium to medium-fast."[17] As the service progresses, the tempo is slowed down again. In Wimber's words, "Usually slow, like a sweet and gentle ballad. . . . God's presence in these settings sometimes reaches great intensity. It seems we can only endure so much . . . as though God would press us into the floor."[18]

Then in this further manipulation by music, the instruments and singers will lead the people into music in which "tempo can be medium-fast to very fast, danceable songs are best."[19]

Now in all the above, something else is taking place within the structure—the pitch varies with the tempo. I will not explore this further. Suffice it to say at this point, the people are systematically mesmerized through music. (Please see chapter 12 for mesmerism.)

In all this, I believe Wimber knows exactly what he is advocating. After all, he had been a professional musician. He says in *Power Evangelism*:

> [I was] eventually moving on to involvement with bands with national exposure and a few that even gained international attention. By 1962, my career was soaring. I worked with several bands, such as a Las Vegas show group and a rock-and-roll group called the Righteous Brothers.[20]

I call all this *emotional control*. I was familiar with it before I became a Christian, when I promoted dances to raise enough money to finance my drug habit. There are many things that we continue to do as Christians, after our salvation, such as eating and sleeping. But there are some things that must be forsaken. One of them is manipulation. It comes in many forms. But no matter the shape it takes, the victim becomes a slave to the manipulator, unless the victim deliberately decides to take an alternate course.

When I accepted a pastorate in Canada's national capital many years ago, a man in the church came to me and said, "Pastor, you need a new suit. Would you be offended if I bought you one?" He had already arranged with a tailor to measure me. I praised God! I needed a new suit very badly.

Then while wearing my new suit, another man from another church came to me and said, "Pastor, you need a new suit." All the while he was rubbing my back with one hand and holding my elbow with his other hand. He was trying to manipulate me.

The first man never asked for a favor. The second one did in less than two weeks. And I would have been glad to assist him without my new suit.

Returning to Wimber's *Worship Experience* notes we learn that next comes "the Expression of Ecstasy."[21] According to him, this is the stage in which "the worshipper is taken into heights of joy. . . . In the Vineyard, we visit this place only occasionally: usually in conference settings after three to five days." Then Wimber cautions, "The experience is more rare at home . . . lest we find ourselves in a frenzied, counterfeit experience. . . . To reach this stage, we must take the risk of looking and sounding foolish before God and men."[22]

And I ask, "Why?"

Wimber gives no reason for his statement.

We are now at Wimber's fourth step in emotional control through music. A direct quote from Wimber's writing will help to clarify what he means: "Tempo can be medium-fast to very fast, danceable songs are best.[23] . . . The presence of God's Spirit is strong, and intensifies.[24] . . . The only law governing worship is the law of love.[25] . . . The things which we control, God uses very little."[26]

"The only law governing worship is the law of love."[27] How can a man so knowledgeable in the Scriptures make such a statement? John 4:24 says something completely different: "God is spirit; and those who worship Him *must* worship in spirit and truth" (italics mine).

Then he goes on to say, "The things which we control, God uses very little."[28] Yet all the while he is giving us "teaching" on how to control a worship service. I would have to respond by saying, "When we have self-control, God *can* use us!" (See Galatians 5:22-23.)

This then, from his own printed notes, is Wimber's design for controlling Vineyard music. In each of the four steps, he also suggests choruses to be sung. In the listings he provides, he ignores two large areas of biblical admonition: "Be filled with the Spirit, speaking to one another in *psalms* and *hymns* and spiritual songs, singing and making melody" (Ephesians 5:18-19, italics mine).

I have seen Wimber's approach to music used in many meetings, exploiting people who think they are being spiritually blessed. And likely some are genuinely touched by God. However, in many respects, we get the same lift by going to a football game where the home team wins. The

60

game starts off slowly as the teams feel each other out. Then there is scoring. After intermission, the teams regroup and come out with the same uniforms, but with different heart. At the last moment, the home team pulls ahead, and everyone goes home happy.

For a few days, they may retain this feeling of exhilaration. There is no sense of being manipulated. They came to get a thrill, and they got it. But it is emotional, not spiritual. Now there is nothing wrong with emotion. Who among us does not need an emotional lift occasionally? Our church services should provide that, but not just that. We need something more, something that will last beyond a few days! We need a touch from God.

It is not likely that we will experience God without emotion. However, we may be moved emotionally without experiencing God. And I have seen a lot of the latter in recent years.

In a Sunday morning worship service, I witnessed Rev. John Arnott and his worship team implementing Wimber's system to perfection (described further in chapter 10). Has he created a monster that cannot be controlled? It appears to me that he has.

This is the old camp-meeting style. Everything builds up to a certain climax, usually on the last night. People respond. They fall on their knees, weep and laugh. Then they go home with little or no change of life, just waiting for next year. In the above sequence of music manipulation, as detailed in Wimber's seminar, a way has been found to do "camp" in one meeting! I feel strongly that it is not without danger!

In 1994, while ministering in General Santos City, Philippines, I was quite disturbed by a certain Bible college's use of music in the evening meetings. I decided to lecture on the matter in morning chapel. When I stated that what they were doing was encouraging demonic activity, my message was received with considerable doubt.

That evening the music was even more demon-enticing, as the musicians followed an approach similar to Wimber's.[29] As soon as I began to preach, a young lady weighing about ninety pounds started screaming and knocking over people-filled pews.

Students and other adults rallied around, each loudly praying at random—demons love confusion. I had to yell to get people to be quiet. Then the demons were cast out and the lady taken to another room and ministered to, since she was exhausted. At this point, I returned to the pulpit and casually asked all those who had attended chapel that morning to please stand. Then I asked all those who still doubted what I had taught in chapel to please raise their hands. No one did.

It has become widely known that the Toronto Airport Christian Fellowship does not do exorcism, preferring rather to concentrate on "simply receiving."[30] I give examples of this issue later, in chapters 8 and 10.

Upon reading Wimber's model for the worship experience, Dr. Rivard noted that the concept

> is narrow in its careful orchestration to produce a desired public response, because not everyone speaks this worship language. The Scriptures record several ways in which Jesus worshiped the Father, including private prayer and public synagogue attendance. All were intimate experiences. I am concerned that some worshipers may be tempted to pretend, displaying the public response that they are encouraged to do. Who knows? God may choose to be silent today. Although we can be manipulated, He cannot.[31]

The problem with the Vineyard system is that it is designed

> to produce an effect. The same effect every time. "If you sing certain songs certain ways you will be intimate with God and experience ecstasy." If you don't, have you worshipped? What if God is silent? Will you have to pretend He responded in order to keep the ball rolling?[32]
>
> This type of service relies on the premise that God only speaks one way, and it is up to us to get Him to speak that way. But that is false.[33]

Ron and Patricia Owens have had a music ministry for many years and know something of the power music wields. Concerning the Toronto Blessing, Ron says, "They raised people to an adrenaline high that not only had them dancing, but also climbing on chairs around me. They were then gradually let down only to be crescendoed to another high."[34]

What Ron Owens observed at the Airport Vineyard is exactly what Wimber has taught in his lecture paper from which we have been quoting. And it is exactly what I observed in a variety of services at TACF. I will discuss these observations in later chapters.

> Once it was my working, His it hence
> shall be;
> Once I tried to use Him, Now He
> uses me;
> Once the power I wanted, Now the
> Mighty One;
> Once for self I labored, Now for Him
> alone.[35]

Endnotes

1. Brian Doerksen, *Worship Songs of the Vineyard*, Vol. 2 (Anaheim, CA: Vineyard Ministries International, 1991), p. 34.

2. Eugene Rivard, unpublished notes, March 1996.

3. F.A. Norwood, "Charles Wesley," *The World Book Encyclopedia*, Vol. 21, p. 163.

4. John Wimber, unpublished notes, *The Worship Experience*, Section 15, p. 171ff, as taught by Gary Best in Edmonton, Alberta, January 1990.

5. Ibid., p. 179.

6. Ibid.

7. Ibid., p. 172.

8. Ibid.

9. Ione Loewan, *Non-Christian Religions* (Wheaton, IL: Van Kampen Press, n.d.), pp. 53f.

10. Rivard, unpublished notes.

11. Eugene Rivard, in reply to Robert J. Kuglin letter, March 4, 1996.

12. Wimber, p. 173.

13. Ibid.

14. Ibid., p. 175.

15. Ibid.

16. Ibid., p. 172.

17. Ibid., p. 176.

18. Ibid., pp. 177-178.

19. Ibid., p. 181.

20. John Wimber, *Power Evangelism* (London: Hodder and Stroughton, 1985), p. 14.

21. Wimber, *The Worship Experience*, p. 179.

22. Ibid., p. 180.

23. Ibid., p. 181.

24. Ibid., p. 182.

25. Ibid.

26. Ibid., p. 183.

27. Ibid., p. 182.

28. Ibid., p. 183.

29. Ibid., p. 171f.

30. "The Fifth Estate," Canadian Broadcasting Corporation, January 1996, available on video cassette.

31. Rivard, unpublished notes.

32. Ibid.

33. Ibid.

34. Ron Owens, "The Toronto Revival," Special Report, Winter 1995, *Prayer and Spiritual Awakening,* Home Mission Board, Southern Baptist Convention, p. 2.

35. A.B. Simpson, "Himself," *Hymns of the Christian Life* (Camp Hill, PA: Christian Publications, 1978), #248.

Chapter 6

Catch the Fire

I like books—new books, old books, unusual books. That is obviously one reason why I felt drawn to Guy Chevreau's *Catch the Fire*. Mr. Chevreau uses fully one-third of his 225-page book to investigate the writings and ministry of Jonathan Edwards (1703-1758).[1] Edwards has been described as a philosopher, preacher, revivalist and theologian who became the leading intellectual figure in colonial America.[2]

Another reason for my keen interest comes from my experience as a soul winner, a pastor and an evangelist for nearly half a century. I have prayed many times that some of my fellow workers would "catch the fire." Too often Christian workers have resorted to secular methods to build up the Body of Christ. This has resulted in decisions without repentance. And without repentance there is no salvation.

One of my co-laborers in the Orient, upon returning from a mission in America, remarked, "It is amazing what the American church has been able to accomplish without God." That terrible indictment has been my observation also. How refreshing it is to read about Holy Spirit revivals, both past and present.

Historically Chevreau is well qualified to write about Jonathan Edwards and how Edwards might view the Toronto Blessing. A Toronto lad, he became a Christian in 1972 through the ministry of Young Life.[3] He received his Doctor of Theology degree from Wycliffe College, Toronto, majoring in historical theology,[4] after struggling through a short pastorate in the province of New Brunswick.[5]

I can almost feel his pain as he speaks of "reaching people from the pulpit" with his "introduction, three points and a poem," as he was taught in seminary.[6] Amazingly enough, when I began to lay aside such man-made ideas and give messages like Peter's and Stephen's, the Lord began working through His Word. What a contrast from my previous experience! Now it was God working through me, rather than me doing the work. Consequently I certainly could understand Chevreau's feelings.

While church planting a Convention Baptist church in what is called "The Golden Horseshoe" in Ontario, Chevreau finally decided to quit. He wrote:

> The winter of '94 was one of the most demanding periods of my life, and left me feeling like I'd been "ridden hard and put away wet." By early May it was

obvious that the work would not be viable, and we terminated the mission the following month.[7]

By a casual reading of the account, it sounds like the church died a natural death. However, a closer look at the situation creates a different scenario. Chevreau and his wife Janis had been in touch with the Toronto Airport Vineyard during this time, and some unusual events soon took place in the Chevreau home.

He says in a 1994 Vineyard tape, "I was too desperate to be skeptical. I was planting an Oakville church but it wasn't pretty."[8] In his book he says,

> I came, more desperate than curious, and too desperate to be critical. . . . We saw uncontrollable laughter and inconsolable weeping; violent shaking and falling down; people waving their arms around, in windmill-like motions, or vigorous judo-like chopping with their forearms.
>
> Janis . . . was down on the floor, repeatedly, hysterical with laughter. At one point, John Arnott . . . prayed that she would stay in this state for forty-eight hours . . . unable to walk a straight line, certainly unfit to drive, or to host the guests that came for dinner the next evening. . . . When I asked after [about] the meal, Janis nearly fell to

the floor in hysterical laughter. I went out to buy fish and chips. . . .

On my return our guests were already seated at the table. Without any place settings, Janis proceeded to toss hot, greasy fish to each of us; she dumped the box of french fries in the middle of the table, and then pushed little piles in our respective directions.[9]

The next evening I came forward for prayer. I "went down," yielding to the feelings of weakness and heaviness. With no cognitive or emotive content, I lay there. . . . Did I get pushed? I came forward [a second time] in a bad mood. Again I went down and . . . I said, "God, I don't care if this is You or not.". . . The third time . . . as I lay there, I started weeping. Wailing, if the truth be told, for something like forty minutes . . . "resting in the Spirit" . . . as my body shook uncontrollably while lying there.[10]

Note the words "desperate" and "hysterical" in the above abbreviated account. These can get a person into very serious difficulty. Did the Convention Baptist Church he was attempting to plant die a natural death? Or were there some extenuating circumstances? A revived pastor generally means a revived church. But his Oakville church died.

Chevreau, who joined the Airport pastoral staff, says further, "While the physical manifestations . . . are abundant and varied, we have endeavored to shift the focus off them."[11] Yet by late 1995 these physical manifestations had escalated to a fever pitch, so much so that they became one of the main reasons for the dismissal from Vineyard.[12] Perhaps by then they had decided they *were* essential.

I find it strange that Chevreau feels it necessary to go back to the 1700s in an effort to get support for the happenings at the Airport Church, and also to find a man who showed considerable discernment. While Jonathan Edwards was, indeed, a master concerning revivals and discernment, there have been many since that time. But when similarly Spirit-endowed people come to the fore today to talk or write about present-day happenings, Chevreau classes them among the resisters and antagonists.[13]

In the seventy-five pages that Chevreau devotes to Edwards, he quotes passages like the following:

> . . . extraordinary affections, accompanied by physical demonstrations of fear, sorrow, love, joy; of tears, trembling, groans, loud outcries, agonies of body, and the failing of bodily strength, of fits, jerks and convulsions. . . . [T]he congregation was frequently in tears, some weeping with sorrow and distress, others with joy and love, others with

pity and concern for neighbors. . . .
Their joyful surprise has caused their
hearts as it were to leap, so that they
have been ready to break forth into
laughter, tears often at the same time is-
suing like a flood, and intermingling
with loud weeping.[14]

Catch the Fire also dwells on the experiences of
Mrs. Sarah Edwards.

The presence of God was so near, and
so real, that I seemed scarcely conscious
of anything else. I continued in a sweet
and lively sense of divine things . . . of
God's infinite grace, and favor, and love
to me . . . a sweet and lively exercise.[15]

To this, many of my readers would give a resounding "praise the Lord." However,
Chevreau, in the myriad of quotations from Edwards, is caught in a trap of his own making.
He is quoting Edwards to prove that the Airport Vineyard has validation for its physical
manifestations. But nowhere does he quote Edwards as even mentioning animal and bird
noises, let alone condoning them. And there
have been plenty of such noises in the Toronto
Blessing.

Indeed, Edwards gives some very plain rules
about how to handle manifestations, without any
reference to dogs, lions, cows or kangaroos. He

bases his concerns on First John 4:1: "Beloved, do not believe every spirit, but test the spirits to see whether they are from God; because many false prophets have gone out into the world." There were nine features that he called "no-signs." Edwards says that these nine should not be used either positively or negatively to determine true revival. They are as follows:

1. That the work is carried on in an unusual way.
2. That it produces strong effects on the bodies of participants.
3. That it prompts a great deal of noise (attention).
4. That it stirs people's imaginations.
5. That it is promoted too much by the influence of example and testimony.
6. That it results in imprudent conduct.
7. That errors of judgment and even delusions of Satan are intermingled with it.
8. That some of its professed converts later fall into scandal.
9. That its preachers insist too much on the terrors of God's wrath.[16]

Following his "no-signs," Edwards then states that there are five luminous signs that a revival is truly of God:

1. It raises people's esteem of Jesus as Son of God and the Savior of the world.

2. It leads them to turn away from sin and toward holiness.
3. It increases their love for the Bible.
4. It grounds them in the basic truths of the faith.
5. It evokes greater love for and service to God and other people.[17]

Mr. Chevreau also stretches a point in his references to the Edwardses to suit purpose and audience. While the narrative merely says that Mrs. Edwards was in the sweet presence of God for four hours, Chevreau says in his tape to pastors that "she is overcome and falls face first into her Bible,"[18] becoming the longest quiet time she has had! Much laughter ensues, of course. Another time when a visitor began talking of the glories of the hereafter, Mrs. Edwards had again become "greatly affected." Chevreau says on his tape, "She fell face first into her mashed potatoes."[19] Did he inject this to try to condone his own wife's actions in the distribution of the fish and chips?

Chevreau uses twelve pages to draw a parallel between the criticisms of the Toronto Blessing to that of Charles Chauncy during the days of Edwards.[20] I think there is a great difference. By no stretch of the imagination could Chauncy be called an evangelical. He was the leading Congregationalist minister in Boston, who not only attacked Edwards, but also other such evangelicals as the renowned George Whitefield.[21] In his later years, Chauncy gave leadership to the Unitarians.[22]

In our day, Dr. John Stott would be considered on an intellectual par with Edwards. In an interview for *Christianity Today* (January 8, 1996), Dr. Stott was asked, "What do you make of the Toronto Blessing?" He replied:

> I never want to criticize anything which people claim has been a blessing to them in terms of a greater awareness of the reality of God, or a profounder of joy, or an overwhelming love for God and for others, or a fresh zeal in evangelism. It's not for me to doubt any of these things.
>
> My major questions concern three areas. First, it is a self-consciously anti-intellectual movement. I listened on tape to the first person who brought the Toronto Blessing to Britain. This person said, "Don't analyze, don't ask questions. Simply receive." I think that is both foolish and dangerous. We must never forget that the Holy Spirit is the Spirit of truth.
>
> Secondly, I cannot possibly come to terms with those animal noises, and it grieves me very much that—as far as I know—no charismatic leaders have publicly disassociated themselves from them, as they should. The whole Bible

tells us that we are different from the animal creation; it rebukes us when we behave like animals and calls us to be distinct. Nebuchadnezzar's animal behavior was under the judgment, not the blessing, of God.

My third problem concerns all the falling. Even charismatic leaders have pointed this out, that on the few occasions in the Bible when people have fallen over, they have all fallen forward on their faces, and they have all done so *after* they have been granted a vision of the majesty, holiness, and the glory of God. In the Toronto experience, however, people fall backwards without any previous vision of God. These three things trouble me.[23]

And I would add that they also trouble me.

Chevreau gives a number of examples of writings from past centuries. There are few readers that are able to validate what he has written or would take the time to analyze what the original authors were saying. At random, I have selected the French clergyman, Hilary of Poiters, whose writing Chevreau uses to show that the phenomena at the Toronto Blessing have been going on for centuries. Writing from AD 356 to 367, Hilary comments on John 7:37-38: "If any man is thirsty, let him come to Me and drink. He who believes in Me, as the Scripture said,

'From his innermost being shall flow rivers of living water.' "

Consider the points of error as Hilary explains this Scripture. He wrote:

> When we receive the Holy Spirit, we are made drunk. Because out of us, as a source, various streams of grace flow, the prophet prays that the Lord will inebriate us. The prophet wants the same persons to be made drunk . . . so that their generation may be multiplied. This means that the good earth is compared in the gospel simile to the seed of the word. . . . We who have been reborn through the sacrament of baptism experience intense joy.[24]

Obviously, Hilary was not an evangelical. He states that the sacrament of baptism equals the "born again" experience that Jesus doubly emphasized in the third chapter of John: "I say to you, unless one is born again, he cannot see the kingdom of God. Do not marvel that I said to you, 'You must be born again' " (John 3:3, 7).

Nowhere in the two accounts of the parable of the sower is there an indication that the "good earth" is the seed of the Word. Let the reader turn to Matthew 13:18-23 and Luke 8:4-15. Instead of "don't analyze, don't ask questions, simply receive," as recommended by Airport speakers, I advise that you do analyze, question and only receive truth. Be like the Bereans in Acts 17:10-11, whom Paul called "noble" for examining the Scriptures "to see whether these things were so."

Hilary also says that the prophet wants the people to be drunk.[25] Let me draw to the attention of the reader that the speaker was not merely a prophet; He was the Lord Jesus Christ. And there is absolutely nothing in the passage to say He wanted the people drunk. For Chevreau to go back centuries and use heretical teaching to try to prove a point is appalling, especially for a man with a doctorate in theology who claims to be an evangelical. Such attempted vindication for the unique manifestations associated with the Toronto Blessing is questionable to say the least.

O souls that are seeking for pleasure,
    Your follies and pleasures pursue;
Contend for the prizes of fortune,
    Such trifles may answer for you.
But mine is a nobler ambition;
    I seek for a richer reward;
I want to be Christlike and holy;
    I want to be just like my Lord.[26]

Endnotes

1. Guy Chevreau, *Catch the Fire* (Toronto: Harper-Collins, 1994), pp. 70-144.

2. William A. Clebsch, "Jonathan Edwards," *The World Book Encyclopedia*, vol. 6 (Chicago: Field Enterprises Educational Corporation, 1973), p. 76.

3. Chevreau, p. 3.

4. Ibid., p. ix.

5. Ibid., p. 4.

6. Ibid.

7. Ibid., p. 12.

8. Airport Vineyard Ministries, Tape 1, January 1994.

9. Chevreau, pp. 13-14.

10. Chevreau, pp. 14-15.

11. Ibid., p. viii.

12. See chapter 17.

13. Chevreau, pp. 71, 97.

14. Ibid., pp. 90-91, 93.

15. Ibid., pp. 76-77.

16. Jonathan Edwards, *The Great Awakening*, ed. C.C. Coen, vol. 4 (New Haven, CT: The Yale University Press, 1972), pp. 228-248.

17. Ibid., pp. 248-259.

18. Airport Vineyard Ministries, Tape 1, January 1994.

19. Ibid.

20. Chevreau, pp. 97, 111-115.

21. Garth M. Rosell and Richard A.G. Dupuis, eds., *The Memoirs of Charles G. Finney: The Complete Restored Text* (Grand Rapids, MI: Zondervan, 1989), p. 369, footnote 54.

22. William De Arteaga, *Quenching the Spirit* (Altamonte, FL: Creation House, 1992), p. 53.

23. John Stott, quoted in *Christianity Today*, January 8, 1996.

24. Howard Snyder, *Signs of the Spirit* (Grand Rapids, MI: Zondervan, 1989), quoted in *Catch the Fire*, pp. 218-219.

25. Chevreau, p. 219, quoting Hilary.

26. A.B. Simpson, "I Want to Be Holy," *Hymns of the Christian Life* (Camp Hill, PA: Christian Publications, 1978), #235.

Chapter 7

A Broad View

Two thousand people waited to receive their blessing.

> Many were soon screaming, laughing and writhing uncontrollably. Hundreds simply keeled over. Others howled and barked like farmyard animals, and most lost all co-ordination. It was, at times, like a mass meeting at the Ministry of Silly Walks.[1]

The Toronto Airport Christian Fellowship? No. This was Telford, England, where John Arnott had taken the Toronto Blessing, as reported in England's *Sunday Telegraph* on February 6, 1996.

> Not long ago the power of God fell on a Canadian congregation. Hundreds of men and women of all sorts were so powerfully moved by preaching and prayers

that they wept, laughed, trembled, roared, and collapsed, "slain in the Spirit." Some converted to Christianity; others returned to the faith they had forsaken; and many more were strengthened in the faith they already had.[2]

The Toronto Airport Christian Fellowship? No, not this one either. This was at the Hay Bay Camp Meeting near Kingston, in Central Canada in 1805, as told by George Rawlyk. The main participants were Methodists. But in spite of this great stirring, there is now no longer a Methodist church, as such, in Canada. The Free Methodists are struggling and recently closed their Bible college in Moose Jaw, Saskatchewan. They have only eight foreign missionaries. While the effects of revivals may be felt for many years, to my knowledge no revival has ever gone on for even a decade.

A short while later the showers of blessing descended again. People came from near and far to experience healing, exorcism, speaking in tongues, and exhortations to holy living as all around them men and women swayed and shook, many falling to the ground. Pastors of several denominations came to witness the events and, said one observer, "Many are going away never to be the same again."[3]

The Toronto Airport Christian Fellowship? Wrong again. This is a paragraph from Richard Riss's book, *Survey of Twentieth Century Revival Movements in North America*. It is part of the account of the "Latter Rain" movement in North Battleford in Western Canada in 1948, which was the year I became a Christian. I heard a lot about it as I headed west from Ontario to Canadian Bible College. But I did not understand what was happening and was too proud to show my ignorance by asking anybody.

> That night as we were praying together, suddenly the Holy Spirit came just as He did on the day of Pentecost. As I was sitting next to my sister, I heard this mighty rushing sound. It sounded like a small tornado in the church. . . . Then I heard the fire bell ringing. . . . When they got to the church they saw the flames, but the church wasn't burning. . . . It was the fire of God. Because of this, many people received Christ as their Savior and also the baptism of the Holy Spirit.[4]

One of the laymen stood up at the church described above and quoted some Scriptures and then began to prophesy. Speaking to laymen he said, "Tomorrow you must go out and preach the gospel." In the first three months, they had "about seventy groups of laymen that were going out and preaching the Gospel."[5]

The Toronto Airport Christian Fellowship? No, this was on the Island of Timor. Thus started the great Indonesian Revival in 1965, as recorded in *Like a Mighty Wind* by Mel Tari.

Shortly after reading the book, I asked the Rev. Harold Catto, my long-time friend and field chairman of The Christian and Missionary Alliance in that area, if the unusual accounts of the miraculous were true. He assured me that everything that happened through the Presbyterian Church on Timor—walking on water, a light leading men through the jungle at night, the dead raised, water turned to wine, physical healings—had been validated.

Here is another account:

> As I entered . . . people were lying all over the floor, in various positions. Some had their feet in the air, laughing uncontrollably. Intermingled among the laughing was roaring like lions (some people on all fours, some sitting). I observed one growling man, on all fours, facing a seated woman who was pointing at him and laughing uncontrollably. Stepping around the bodies, I saw several who were jerking (violently shaking). I carefully made my way through this scene to a standing group of people who were waiting for the auditorium doors to open.[6]

So writes Ron Owens in his winter 1995 report on "Prayer and Spiritual Awakening," presented to the Home Mission Board of the Southern Baptist Convention. It was what he "encountered in the lobby of the Constellation Conference Centre" in Toronto. "It was the final service of a Catch the Fire Conference, sponsored by the church and national Vineyard leadership. There were, I was told, about 3,000 in attendance from all over the world."[7] I have read other accounts of up to 6,000 in attendance. *Christian Week* uses 5,500 in its February 13, 1996 issue.[8]

> The service started. . . . Backed by various instruments, a singer began singing:
>
> > "On the floor again, on the floor again;
> > > With my friends again, on the floor again;
> > Who will be there with me as I lie tonight,
> > > On the floor again?"
>
> After a few minutes' break, the musicians began again. They were now singing an upbeat-tempo song about the Holy Spirit that had everyone on their feet clapping and dancing. Then, just as suddenly as they had begun, they stopped, and the lead singer shouted, "Aha! We fooled you!" And everybody

laughed, and laughed and laughed. . . . They had used the Holy Spirit to play a joke on the people, and the people had joined in the frivolity. . . . [There was] lack of reverence and awe of a holy God. . . . By now the music was getting rather loud.

For the next hour, I observed what I can only describe as a masterful manipulation of human emotions by the music leaders. . . . They raised the people to an adrenaline high that had them not only dancing, but also climbing on chairs around me. They were then let down only to be crescendoed to another high. . . . The content of the message was very good, but it was interesting to note that many, who had been so full of life a short time earlier, now sat bored. A number got up and left. I counted only four Bibles.

What I saw at invitation time grieved the Spirit in me. So much was done to generate a response. A woman who was introduced as being a leading prophetess was asked to admonish the people. In the middle of this [very serious time for decisions] she whispered something in the speaker's ear that brought laughter from both of them.[9]

And laughter generates laughter.

Yes. This is the Toronto Blessing! This is what has been happening through the workings of the former Toronto Airport Vineyard. Note the differences in all the above quoted "revivals." One might well ask, "Which is revival and which is not?"

Compare the above with the following.

> What has been billed as a spiritual awakening has been credited with an unusual phenomena in Saskatoon [Canada]—a surge of people making up for past dishonesty.
>
> One of the results has been "conscience money" being paid to various places of business in recent days. Another has been the public renouncement by many young people of taking drugs. One man had defrauded the Workman's Compensation Board and was repaying what he owed.
>
> . . . Bob McPherson, manager of the Zellers' Country Fair, said two persons confessed to stealing from his store. . . . One was on welfare and offered to repay a portion from each cheque (check). Another admitted theft, and offered to work, free of charge, to pay for what was taken.
>
> Frank Hammond, manager of Simpson Sears, said two persons appeared recently wanting to pay for stolen property. A store employee paid money

into the lunchroom coffee fund for coffee he had taken without paying.

The Sutera crusade was extended . . . with 2,800 persons attending.[10]

All this and much more was reported in the Saskatoon *Star Phoenix*, November 12, 1971.

Then from the Regina *LeaderPost*, November 24, 1971 came this account:

> The Sutera Twins . . . drew 200 people to Ebenezer Baptist Church . . . moved to St. James Anglican Church and then to University Drive Alliance Church with a capacity of 1,700 a night and the largest church facility in Saskatoon.
>
> People stand up . . . to tell of repaying old debts [the story is becoming legend among Saskatoon store keepers], renewing friendships, making up with spouse and children. "People right with God can help other people," said Lou. . . . "This is group therapy with Christ as the focal point," said Ralph.
>
> About 40 percent of the crowd were young people representing every walk of life and from many denominations. The twins have no magical touch. People . . . have returned to their own churches and initiated their own New Testament Christianity.

> Honesty and love for fellow man is the general theme of the service which is the "only thing that is going to save the world from moral decay."[11]

The overall impact on Canada was widely felt. It sent me to Florida and Georgia and eventually "to the ends of the earth." The University Drive Alliance soon became the 3,000-seat Circle Drive Alliance. Canadian Bible College/Theological Seminary jumped in attendance from 190 students to nearly 600 in only a few years. The Canadian Revival Fellowship was born, and as I write, it is celebrating its twenty-fifth anniversary. But as I have already noted, revivals are not necessarily long-lived. Present trends of "ups and downs" are consistent with scriptural patterns.

During the reigns of David and Solomon, there was an "up" period. Then came Rehoboam who appointed false priests, bringing in a "down" time. Following times of war under Abijah, Asa brought in a reformation. It was an "up" time. Then under Ahab there came another "down" time.

In this chapter, we have looked at "revival" in general with examples from around the world as well as from the Toronto Airport Christian Fellowship. Now let the reader make an intelligent choice, with the gift of wisdom which is available to us all, basing that choice on Scripture and the product produced.

Send divine conviction, Bring salvation
    nigh;
Crucify and quicken, Save and sanctify.
Blessed Spirit, bring us Power from on
    high.[12]

Endnotes

1. *The Toronto Globe,* February 7, 1996, quoting Tim Reid from the *Sunday Telegraph,* London, England, on February 6, 1996.

2. George A, Rawlyk, *The Canada Fire: Radical Evangelicalism in British North America, 1775-1812,* (Montreal: McGill-Queen's University Press, 1944).

3. Richard Riss, *A Survey of Twentieth Century Revival Movements in North America* (Peabody, MA: Hendrickson Pubs., Inc., 1988).

4. Mel Tari, *Like a Mighty Wind,* (Carol Stream, IL: Creation House, 1971), pp. 24-25.

5. Ibid., pp. 28-29.

6. Ron Owens, "The Toronto Revival," *Special Report,* Winter 1995, "Prayer and Spiritual Awakening," Home Mission Board, Southern Baptist Convention, p. 2.

7. Ibid.

8. Sue Careless, *The Christian Week,* February 13, 1996, p. 1.

9. Owens, p. 2.

10. "Renewed Morality Found in Wake of Revival," Saskatoon *Star Phoenix,* November 12, 1971, p. B-1.

11. "Evangelists Drawing Large Crowds," Regina *LeaderPost*, November 24, 1971, p. 27.

12. A.B. Simpson, "Power from on High," *Hymns of the Christian Life* (Camp Hill, PA: Christian Publications, 1978), #249.

Chapter 8

A Typical
Toronto Blessing Service

I entered the new home of the Toronto Airport Christian Fellowship about an hour before service time. I wanted to be sure of both a parking spot and a good seat to observe everything that would happen. I also wanted to note anything that might occur before the service began.

People were milling around, but I was welcomed by absolutely no one, not even the welcome table personnel. I watched the worship team practice for a while and then headed into the cafeteria for a snack. I was completely ignored there too, except by the cashier, who looked as though she had never smiled in her thirty-or-so years. All this belied the message of the multilingual banners which boldly proclaimed, "To walk in God's love and give it away."

Shortly before service time, I returned to my seat which I had reserved by placing my coat on it. People started taking their places in the 2,000-seat auditorium as the worship team began to perform. What a change! Without an audience, they had appeared normal. But now with an audience, some of them were overcome with jerks while others had "belly spasms."

I was informed that the "belly spasms" resulted when people were so filled with the Holy Spirit that they began to have birth pains. It was interesting to note that the men had the birth pains while the women had the jerks. Could this possibly have resulted because John Wimber had announced that God had spoken to him through the scriptural account of Sarah[1]—"And the LORD said to Abraham, 'Why did Sarah laugh, saying, "Shall I indeed bear a child, when I am so old?"'" (Genesis 18:13).

He had also said that the word "pentecost" had come to him twice in the previous year.[2] (It had come to *me* twelve times in that same period as I had read the Bible through four times that year.) It is also referred to as the Feast of Weeks. This all appears to have developed because of a "prophetic theology" instead of being Scripture-based. Now what was happening at the TACF was being described as "greater than Pentecost."

I have a mild aversion to the singing part of the service being referred to as *the* "worship time." We also worship God with our tithes and offerings, the reading of the Word, prayer and preaching, to say nothing of quiet meditation in response to the Word—"cease striving and know that I am God" (Psalm 46:10).

The Vineyard singing system, as explained in chapter 5, came into operation. Some good choruses were sung, but no psalms or hymns, just spiritual songs: "Mercy is falling like sweet spring rain [repeated three times], Hey, ho, I receive your mercy, I will dance forever more."[3]

Over and over again. Pick up the tempo. Raise the pitch. Increase the volume.

The progression was quite noticeable. Raising of hands, then clapping. Clapping louder, then swaying. Then dancing and jumping which they called "pogoing." A frail little old lady was jumping two feet high. Some of the badge-wearing "ministry team," being younger, jumped even higher. It is interesting to note that the women pogoed, but the men did not. Some of the men fell on all fours making animal noises, but not singing. Almost the whole congregation was out of control, or rather, under the control of the musicians and singers. This went on for almost an hour.

The singing was the part called worship. All else came under a different category. It appears that the larger the crowd, the easier it is to manipulate. On this particular night, with less than 300 in attendance, manipulation appeared to be more difficult than when the church was full.

Earlier I had noticed a young lady take her place near the front at the middle aisle. As she was seated, the people in front and behind her moved to another area. So did the people seated to her left. Having been a minister for so many years, I sensed something was planned. This lady, wearing a "ministry team" badge, began to conduct with her hands, then progressed to ballet. Being rather long-limbed, she needed lots of room to worship. Apparently she was quite oblivious to anyone or anything around her, including the music, since there was no coordination between her dancing and the worship team.

I thought, *It's a good thing all Christians do not have the same gift. We would need church buildings ten times the size just to accommodate a few people who need to "worship" like that.*

Then it was time for the Bible reading. Obligingly the worship team slowed the people down until the clapping, shouting and dancing ceased, although a few "animals" still roamed. In the relative calm of the moment, laughter broke out. The Bible reader joined in. Finally the Bible was laid on the lectern without being read, and a lady from Pittsburgh was called up to testify.

Spontaneity was no longer allowed. Called by name and dressed in slacks, as counseled earlier in the day, she broke into uncontrollable laughter as she tried to tell of her particular deliverance. She had lived in the fear of being killed. She was told that this was prophetic. Now the Holy Spirit would "kill" her. Nearly everybody was in hysterics at this point.

The leader put his hand on her forehead. The male catchers came running and she was "laid to rest" on one side of the platform. She remained there for the rest of the service, often breaking into uncontrollable laughter, as ladies sat with their hands on her. They were said to be "soaking her in the Holy Spirit."

While this was going on, a man charged onto the platform yelling, "Jesus is my father! Jedus is my father! Judas is my father!" These three statements were repeated over and over. The first blasts seemed acceptable to the ushers and they did not respond until the final exclamations. Right from the first outburst, however, he appeared demonic to me. It was when he tore up a little booklet and threw it all around that the ushers came rushing to accost him. He was taken out of the church and left to fend for himself.

He was probably one of the most needy people in the building. He had come right into their midst, but there was no effort to see this young man delivered although he was obviously under Satan's power. The scene seemed to fit what Wes Trotman noted on the TV program, "Fifth Estate"—that the Airport Church did not do exorcism. To refute this John Arnott merely responded that Trotman is a Baptist and that Baptists do not even believe in demon possession.[4]

As the meeting progressed it became clear that the leaders were more interested in getting the believers "under the power" or "anointed" than they were in seeing people redeemed and delivered from sin, self and Satan.

A woman from New York state, who had attended the Rodney Howard-Browne meetings in Albany a year earlier, was called forward by name. Her first words were, "I'll have a hard time beating that last performance." Then she went on to testify that she had been delivered from "wanting to be noticed." She rambled on and on, going from one subject to another. At one point she said she was from Albany, a city so hard that even Finney wouldn't preach there. However, I notice in Finney's memoirs that he preached there with Rev. Edward N. Kirk, pastor of the Fourth Presbyterian Church, "for some weeks."[5] She also said she had lived in Utica, which was also so hard that Finney did not preach there. But Finney gives a whole chapter of the same book to the Utica revival.[6]

Finally the catchers were summoned as the chairman said she needed some more "soaking." If that would help, I thought she needed more too. He gave her a little push on the forehead and down she went, taking her male and female catchers with her. They spread her out on the opposite side of the platform from the first lady, where she remained for the rest of the meeting.

A pastor from the Reformed Church in Switzerland was called to testify. He received a big hand from the people. As he attempted to speak, he bent over with severe pain in the abdomen. He was told that this was prophetic. He would be giving birth to a new church. Many in the congregation of less than 300 began to have the pains as well. Some were in agony. Others laughed. Haltingly this formerly fluent speaker told how all this came to him as he was doing "carpet time" at the previous meetings. I wondered, *Are all those people who are having the same pains as this European pastor to start new churches as well?*

As a speech it was a very sorry performance, but the people were shouting glories to the Holy Spirit. Then the chairman said, "He needs more soaking." And the process was repeated. But this time there wasn't room on the small platform, the ladies having usurped the space. So they dragged him off to the main floor, right in front of me. He was obviously "out." When he aroused, he straightened his clothes, got into a more comfortable position and remained there like the others, "soaking in the Spirit" and missing the sermon. The latter wasn't such a bad idea.

Each of the three would move from time to time into different positions of comfort. This was clearly well planned. It was a primer for others to do likewise later in the evening. Throughout the week, I observed that each service was the same—three people "slain in the Spirit," generally well-placed, one at each side of the lectern and one in front.

Then, with the examples on the floor, came a short, pithy message from First John 2. I would not be fair to my readers if I did not comment on the sermon. The speaker from a nearby Vineyard church said, "People criticize the lack of control. Control is a conditioned response. When you get 'it' through soaking and carpet time, 'it' releases the conditioning, and you do not have control."

And, of course, this is what I saw—people out of control. It is claimed that they are drunk in the Spirit, but this is far removed from the teaching of Scripture. The Bible includes drunkenness in the long line of the works of the flesh in Galatians 5:19-21. And right after this, the Holy Spirit gives us the fruit of the Spirit, the last piece being self-control. Surely the speaker, supposedly knowledgeable in the Word of God, should have known this.

There was another alarming thing. While the ministering team and the worship team could really "whoop it up" during the singing, some of them actually went to sleep during the message while others merely looked bored. Could they have played themselves out while waiting on the Lord, even though the Bible says, "Those who wait for the LORD will gain new strength; they will mount up with wings like eagles. They will run and not get tired, they will walk and not become weary" (Isaiah 40:31)?

The preacher also said, "Most missionaries last only four years. They remain as little children who still need to play." The speaker obviously needed this type of illustration to explain carpet time. My experience was the opposite. Missionaries that I know are career missionaries serving a lifetime.

Carpet time was described as our heavenly Father rolling on the floor with His little children—"He puts us down to play with us." Did the missionaries need to come home to "play" with the Father? This is a rather unusual interpretation of falling on our faces in awe before a holy God.

It appeared that the lady to the right of the lectern had had enough of that kind of preaching. She got up and went to the rest room. But she came back and resumed her position, wailing once in a while.

Perhaps it is time for a word about laughter, which in itself is not wrong, provided it is over appropriate matters and expressed at appropriate times. Anybody can do it. Laughter causes endorphins to be released in the body. An endorphin is a chemical substance that reduces or eliminates pain, but only temporarily. A terrible scare will do the same thing. A bad fall will relieve the pain of someone suffering from acute arthritis, and even put the disease into temporary remission, according to my family physician, Dr. Joseph J. Persram.

So I find nothing wrong with the laughter. We all need it. The Bible says, "A joyful heart is good medicine, but a broken spirit dries up the bones" (Proverbs 17:22). I have seen some professing Christians whose faces tell us, "I haven't laughed in years." For them a good belly-laugh might indeed be refreshing, but to make laughter a focal point of our worship or to call it renewal is stretching things far out of proportion.

There was very little laughter during the actual sermon, although there was the occasional barking. Perhaps this was necessary to alert the many who had wearied themselves during the exhausting, hour-long "worship time." Most seemed to be in stupors. The people were instructed to "not come forward tonight. The teams will minister after the main service at the back of the auditorium."

Before the preaching, there was an altar call for those who needed to be saved. It appeared these were designated before the service. Two ladies were brought forward by workers. A man was called by name a number of times, but refused to come. The preacher took the two ladies through the process of receiving Christ. They were told they must turn their backs on sin and repent, that they must now receive Christ as Savior. They repeated a prayer as directly dictated.

During all this, I was quietly saying, "Praise the Lord!" I did not agree with the methodology, but if two people really repented and took Christ as Savior, there is cause for rejoicing. Since "there will be more more joy in heaven over one sinner who repents" (Luke 15:7), let us rejoice twice as much over two. And might I say to reader and author alike, whether laity or clergy, "Go and do the same" (Luke 10:37).

Then came the hand on the forehead, the catchers behind, and the first lady was "soaking in the presence of the Lord." The team moved to the second lady, but she would not go down. They talked to her, and then tried again and again. The only result was that the large male catcher buckled at the knees. The lady was then taken to a private place for instruction, while the other one remained on the floor.

In this process, there was something that disturbed me. It was the reaction of the congregation. They appeared so passive about souls being saved. But when the one lady went down, they rejoiced with shouts and laughter.

It reminded me of the time I returned home from a crusade and met one of my fellow church elders on the street. "Bob, I didn't know you were home. How did the meetings go?" he asked.

"Great!" I responded and began to recount the work of the Holy Spirit in that place. "Almost the entire village took Christ as Savior. They had even started to build an extension on the church before I left to come home."

"Praise the Lord!" he said, and then asked, "Were there any healings?"

"Oh, yes," I replied. "Besides divine healings, there were some miraculous healings." In my understanding, divine healing is generally gradual, although speeded up, while miraculous healing are instant.

"Hallelujah!" he yelled out and began jumping up and down.

Now I am a little reserved emotionally, but even in my embarrassment while on a busy city street, I had the composure to ask him, "Don't you have your response backward?" He was more excited over healing than he was over conversions. Why is it today that so many of us respond the same way?

Earlier I presented John Wimber's theory of worship experience.[7] It needs to be repeated here. He states that through the manipulation of music "people will fall, shake, experience mass deliverances, healings, salvation, forgiveness, anointing, etc."[8] In the service I observed that music did its part, and the Bible was very briefly preached. Perhaps an acceptable middle ground would have been a little less emotion and a little more Bible.

I have a problem here. What would I prefer? What would you prefer? Here was emotionalism at its apex. And two souls accepted Christ. Is this better than what many others are experiencing through solid Bible exposition, but which is like a T-bone steak served on ice?

After the sermon, the preacher suggested there were people who needed healing. But then he appeared confused as to what should follow. The large male catcher, who had buckled at the knees, stepped forward and motioned to his own left knee. Apparently he had received a revelation. The preacher then called all those with bad left knees to come and be healed.

The frail little old lady, to whom I referred earlier in this chapter, was the first to respond. If she needed her left knee healed, she must certainly have injured it when she took her last leap as she "pogoed" two feet high during the Wimber-style "worship time."

Others came forward, although they had been

told to remain in their seats and the ministering teams would come to them. I found it rather interesting that those who did come forward, also went down to do carpet time. Those who were ministered to without coming forward were not "slain." As I observed a little later, the "slaying" was apparently being reserved until further into the service.

The next invitation was for all those with diabetes to raise their hands. About half the people raised their hands. According to the Canadian Diabetic Association, about one in every twenty people in North America has diabetes in various degrees.[9] Could it be that the proportion is one out of every two in Vineyard? Or did the congregation not understand? Were they still under the control of the music? Had they been so mesmerized that they would respond to anything suggested?

After this, the entire congregation was invited to go to the back of the auditorium. This was obviously a well-known procedure, for without any further instructions, they lined up single file along long strips of red tape on the floor. Almost the whole congregation responded. Then the ministering teams went to work. One prayed, the other caught. One by one the catchers lined them up like cord wood on the floor.

From a show of hands at the beginning of the service over two hours earlier, almost all the people on that particular night were regular attendees. I hoped they were not substituting this for Bible study and prayer.

I went back to my room and read Paul's exhortation in Philippians 4:9—"The things you have learned and received and heard and seen in me, practice these things; and the God of peace shall be with you." I had seen very little in the entire evening of what the Bible teaches. But it certainly had been a demonstration of Wimber-Vineyard techniques. On May 15, 1995 at Trinity TV Complex in Winnipeg, a TACF spokesperson emphasized that "the Bible could not and must not be used to judge the manifestations seen at the Toronto Blessing."[10] To my knowledge, no reason was given for this statement. However, it would appear to be based on the premise that prophetic utterance supersedes the Bible.

I was deeply grieved by the *very* small place given to the Word of God in the meeting. From reading the Bible through so many times, I have noticed the overall emphasis in the Scriptures—that we must give ourselves largely to the use of the Bible itself. I note that in Psalm 119 reference is repeatedly made to walking in, keeping, observing, looking upon, learning, seeking out, treasuring, telling about, rejoicing in, meditating on, regarding, delighting in and living in God's law, testimonies, ways, precepts, statutes, commandments, word, righteous judgments and ordinances. Out of 176 verses, attention is drawn to these things 173 times.

Sprinkled among these verses, the Holy Spirit has given the word "revive" twelve times. Some versions have "quicken." It is one of the overlooked portions of God's Word with regard to revival. And in the Toronto Blessing meetings, the Word of God has been grossly overlooked again. This is not just the observation of one meeting. I was there for one whole week.

I suppose I would be one of those who would be categorized under one of their sayings: "We don't worship the Bible, just the God of the Bible" or "Some people's Trinity is Father, Son and Holy Book."[11]

Later I will comment on some basic thoughts they have inherited on the doctrine of the Trinity.

> Once it was the blessing, Now it is the
> Lord;
> Once it was the feeling, Now it is His
> Word;
> Once His gift I wanted, Now the Giver
> own;
> Once I sought for healing, Now Himself alone.[12]

Endnotes

1. John Goodwin, "Testing the Fruit of the Vineyard," quoting from John Wimber, Healing Seminar Series, audio tapes, Vol. 3, unedited, 1981.

2. Dave Roberts, *The Toronto Blessing* (Eastbourne, Great Britain: Kingsway, 1994), p. 20.

3. From author's notes, copied from the overhead during a Vineyard service. It is said that the Airport musicians make up their own songs.

4. "The Fifth Estate," interviewing Wes Trotman, Canadian Broadcasting Corporation, January 1996, available on video cassette.

5. Garth M. Rosell and Richard Dupuis, eds., *The Memoirs of Charles G. Finney: The Complete Restored Text* (Grand Rapids, MI: Zondervan, 1989), p. 281, footnote 2.

6. Ibid., pp. 172-192.

7. John Wimber, *The Worship Experience,* Section 15, pp. 171ff.

8. Ibid., p. 179.

9. Canadian Diabetes Association, National Office, 78 Bond Street, Toronto, Ontario.

10. Guy Chevreau at a pastor's seminar, Winnipeg, Manitoba, as quoted by Doug Tiffin in a May 16 open letter.

11. Ibid.

12. A.B. Simpson, "Himself," *Hymns of the Christian Life* (Camp Hill, PA: Christian Publications, 1978), #248.

Chapter 9

The Animal in Us

Current activity at the Toronto Airport Christian Fellowship has given new meaning to the old expression, "It's only the animal in him coming out." We once used it to describe a man's fit of anger, his refusal to accept today's equality of roles, his consuming passion for hunting or spending excessive time "with the boys." Today, because of the manifestations at TACF, we must also include the impersonation of animals and birds. Since it is one of the more highlighted events of the movement, no consideration of the Toronto Blessing would be complete without an exploration of this phenomenon.[1]

With Vineyard saying that the animal sounds should be downplayed, it is easy to see why there has been a split—the TACF was allowing the animal phenomena to become the center of attraction. Today it is perhaps a greater "drawing card" than the laughter.

Though proponents of the Blessing claim the phenomena is evidence of the Spirit's power, others do not agree. John Moore of John Moore Evangelistic Association says, "Some of these manifestations also take place in heathen temples and deliverance sessions. . . . People would be wise to test the spirits and see if they are of God."[2] John Arnott responded to Moore's comment by saying, "It's about time the church had more faith in God's ability to bless us than Satan's ability to deceive us."[3] By shifting the focus, Arnott avoids the valid admonition.

In January 1996, he did the same thing on the Canadian Broadcasting Corporation's television show, "Fifth Estate."[4] When Toronto Baptist pastor Wes Trotman suggested there is evidence of demonic activity, Arnott replied, "The Baptists don't even believe in demon possession."[5] He thus avoided the subject. But we will not be too hard on Arnott for this. If I defended myself against all the false accusations thrown at me over the years, I would have had no time to minister. Influential Christian leaders through the years have kept to a philosophy of "Attack not, defend not."

In a March 1994 Airport Vineyard tape, we learn that the speaker, Guy Chevreau, had been away for a number of weeks writing a book. At the time of the recording, he was back at Vineyard to speak to a pastor's conference on Wednesday morning. When he entered the building, four men met him at the door. They were on their hands and knees, roaring like lions, and Chevreau says, "Thank God, I am home again!"[6] If, when listening to the tape, you did not know what it was about, you would think the speaker was a Christian returning to his job at the zoo!

When people heard that I was writing this book and that I had been there for firsthand observations, many asked me about the animal noises. Did I see the manifestations? Did I hear them? What did I think? First let me tell you what I saw and heard, then I will tell you what I think about it all.

I saw a man walking on all fours growling as he went. He nibbled on a few legs. But when he lifted his leg "to claim his territory," in my opinion he had gone much too far. I decided if he came over to me, I would set aside some Christian graces and jar him back to reality. He snarled viciously at me, but went away when I pointed my finger at him and said, "In the name of Jesus . . ." Apparently he did not like that Name. While I was not amused, many people pointed at him and laughed. No wonder one of the books on the Toronto Blessing is entitled *No Laughing Matter*.

Another discovery I made was that human lions roar not only when the sun goes down, but whenever they want attention. They roar while on all fours or on their backs with their feet straight up in the air. It was mostly men who "became" animals. A few women did, but they were more often dancing and speaking in tongues.

John Arnott is quoted in *No Laughing Matter* as saying:

So now we are starting to see people prophetically acting like lions and oxen and eagles and even warriors. . . . It scared some people so bad that many of them ran right out of the meeting. . . . A little keyboard player lady—115 pounds—was on all fours, snorting and pawing the ground like an angry bull. That went on for quite a while and she was frightened. . . . She runs out of the room. Carol [Arnott] went after her. We encouraged her. "You're okay. Just let the Lord do what He wants to do."[7]

To me this sounds more like the judgment of God on Nebuchadnezzar than bringing a special blessing to a young lady.

But rather than dwell on what I refer to as "obscene behavior" by giving further accounts of what I saw, I want to draw from Scripture what God would say about these things. Lions (and lionesses) are mentioned 151 times in the Bible. Dogs, forty times. So it would be impractical to talk about all the verses. But let us turn to the Messianic Psalm 22. It mentions them both in reference to the crucifixion of Jesus, and adds "bulls" for good measure.

Be not far from me, for trouble is near; for there is none to help. Many *bulls* have surrounded me; strong bulls of Bashan have encircled me. They open

wide their mouth at me, as a ravening
and a roaring *lion*. I am poured out like
water, and all my bones are out of joint;
my heart is like wax; it is melted within
me. My strength is dried up like a pot-
sherd, and my tongue cleaves to my
jaws; and Thou dost lay me in the dust
of death. For *dogs* have surrounded me;
a band of evildoers has encompassed
me; they pierced my hands and my feet.
(Psalm 22:11-16, italics mine)

This prophetic psalm uses animal terminology
to describe the actions of people in this very
vivid description of the crucifixion of Jesus.
Wherever the Bible uses an animal to describe a
human, it is always derogatory, except in one
scene. In that one exception Jesus is called "the
Lion that is from the tribe of Judah" (Revelation
5:5). Here the lion is the King of kings.

TACF has said that the roaring is Jesus in the
men yelling out the good news.[8] My own percep-
tion, after randomly speaking to a variety of
Torontonians in hotels, restaurants, gas stations,
taxis and the international airport, is that Christianity has become a very large joke in the
Toronto area. This is completely contrary to
Marc Dupont's prophecies, which were exam-
ined in chapters 2 and 3.

Have I seen people acting like crowing roosters
and gobbling turkeys? Yes, I have. And I have
also heard people claim that little birds are sit-

ting on their shoulders giving them messages and of sick people being ministered to by vultures that perched on the footboards of beds. All of this is anathema. I cannot emphasize this enough. It is terrible.

In our ministry across Canada, my wife and I have recognized demonic forces and had to confront them head-on. On one occasion it involved rooster crowing.

Davie did not belong to our church, but he came to all special events. He would stand and sing with the soloist, but sit and not sing when the congregation did. Davie would not miss a word, even when the soloist sang a new song, which he wrote. This was what some people would call uncanny.

He shouted "amen" and "hallelujah" in the most inappropriate places during the message. I also noticed that he became very uncomfortable when the preacher spoke about Jesus, but he was not bothered when the topic was the Holy Spirit. Demons cannot stand the name of Jesus; naming the Holy Spirit, however, does not seem to affect them.

Davie always avoided me personally. But one day I was able to literally back him into a corner. I told him I would not let him go until he gave me a clear-cut testimony of his salvation. He hedged for a long time, but seeing there was no escape, finally agreed. He took a rigid pose, lifted his chin up high and crowed like a rooster for over fifteen minutes. If I had not seen him do it,

I would have thought there was a mature rooster in the building.

Finally he stopped, returned to his human personality and said, "There!" He caught me off guard and escaped. However, I was not in the custom of proceeding in deliverance ministry when I did not have assistance, so perhaps it was for the best. He never came back to a service again, though I pastored there for seven years.

At the Toronto Blessing, an unnamed lady says her rooster-crowing is prophetic—while "educated theologians cannot recognize it, even a little child would understand."[9] When she crows, she says she is announcing, "There's a new day coming!" Now there will be a new day coming right up to the end of the age. This need not be announced. Since she had become a "professing prophetess," I presume she meant that we were about to enter into a new era of the Holy Spirit.

In the Bible the account of the rooster crowing is in all four Gospels. Of course, it crowed in the morning. That is the nature of the bird. But it did more than announce the morning. It announced to Peter that he had denied the Lord. It was an announcement of a past happening. It was not prophetic. And the rooster was not a human being.

I was asked by a non-Christian if I had talked to the lady that crowed, then he laughed. But it was not the laughter of the "Laughing Revival." It was in derision. The Toronto Blessing, instead of sweeping Toronto in a great revival of repentance and renewal, is bringing the church into disrepute.

While ministering in Dragerton (now called Carbon City), Utah, I was invited, on my rest night, to attend a special meeting in another church. I persuaded my host pastor and his wife to come hear the evangelist and the recording artist who were on their way to Nashville, Tennessee. I told them that they needed to know what was going on in other churches in this small coal mining community.

It was terrible. The auditorium was small and the ceiling was low. Many bodies crowded together made for a very stuffy atmosphere. The singer could sing, but his built-in electronic beat kept accelerating in tempo and pitch. I knew what was happening. The people were wearing down. The leaders could have asked for the response before the preaching and received greater visible results. Music had done its manipulative job, but they were not up on that type of thing. Vineyard had not yet evolved.

The evangelist started off shouting and kept getting louder and louder. He even changed his voice pitch. Then came the altar call. After much pleading a very obese lady went forward and knelt at the altar in her very short skirt. Discretion would not have allowed this. The teenagers loved it.

My friend Richard said, "Let's go." But I grabbed him by the knee and with a very poor choice of words, said, "You haven't seen anything yet." His wife giggled. (This should not be confused with "holy laughter.")

People gathered around the lady. Some laughed. Some cried. Some shouted. Some merely observed. Finally the pastor said, "She has it! She has it!" Everything stopped except the lady who endeavored to get up. Now if she knew how to receive Christ as her Savior, she could be saved under those circumstances. But if she did not know enough to repent and receive Christ, then she was just as lost when they finished as she was before.

The evangelist grabbed her and pushed her back down and blurted out, "Now the gift! Now the gift!" The attendants really "went to it" this time. Quite some time later the lady began to convulse, thrusting her huge body back and forth. Sounds began to issue from her mouth, but her mouth was not formed in the manner of speaking.

With each thrust of her body, she declared, "Gobble! Gobble! Gobble!" If you had not witnessed the scene, you would have been positive that there was a turkey gobbler in church. The evangelist shouted, "She's got it! She's got it!"

I turned to Richard and his wife and said, "I wanted you to see this. Now we can go. She came from her home as a person. Now she goes back as a bird." In my estimation, she went home unconverted and filled with the wrong spirit. I hope I was wrong, but from my years of experience, I do not believe I was.

Then there was the lady in Pennsylvania. She came to me with a big smile and announced, "The Lord has really answered prayer. God has called me to be a traveling evangelist." According to her, the Holy Spirit landed on her shoulder in the form of a bird and gave her this calling.

"That is marvelous," I responded. "That means your husband has accepted the Lord."

She immediately asked, "What has that got to do with it?"

I told her it had a lot to do with it, because nobody would believe her message if she traveled with an unsaved husband.

"Well, I'm going to leave him so I can do what God wants me to do," she said.

I opened my Bible and read to her from First Corinthians 7:13—"And a woman who has an unbelieving husband . . . let her not send her husband away."

She got angry, shut my Bible and said, "I don't care what the Bible says, the Holy Spirit told me to do this." With this, she stomped out of the church.

From my studies, I have concluded that anger stifles the work of the Holy Spirit more decisively than any other sin.

The animals have been with us for a long time. This is no new phenomena. Swami Baba Muktananda

> would transfer what was called "guru grace" to his followers through physical touch (Shaktipat). This "grace" trig-

gered the gradual awakening of the Kundalini which in turn produced various physical and emotional manifestations. These included uncontrollable laughter, roaring, barking, hissing, shaking, etc. Some devotees became mute or unconscious. Many felt themselves being infused with feelings of great joy and peace and love. At other times the "fire" of Kundalini was so overpowering they would find themselves involuntarily hyperventilating to cool themselves down.[10]

Among the good things I saw at Toronto Airport Christian Fellowship, the animal and bird manifestations are certainly not included. Whenever I have faced this type of phenomena in my ministry, I have ended up dealing with demonization.

> Burn in, O fire of God, burn in
>   Till all my soul Christ's image bears
> And every power and pulse within
>   His holy, heavenly nature wears.[11]

Endnotes

1. Larry Thomas, *No Laughing Matter* (Excelsior Springs, MO: Double Crown Publishing, 1995), p. 97, states, "John Wimber compounds the problem by saying there is no scriptural support for such phenomena

and no historial precedent. 'So I feel no obligation to try to explain it. It's just phenomena. It's just people responding to God.' He has said that such behaviors (making animal noises) were considered demonic in the past at his Anaheim Vineyard church."

2. John Moore, *Faith Today*, March-April 1995, p. 19.

3. Ibid.

4. "The Fifth Estate," Canadian Broadcasting Corporation, January 1996, available on video cassette.

5. Ibid.

6. *Airport Vineyard Ministries*, Tape 1, 1994.

7. Thomas, pp. 121-122.

8. Marc Dupont, quoted in *No Laughing Matter*, p. 97.

9. *Airport Vineyard Ministries*, Tape 2, 1994.

10. Danny Aguirre, "Some Examples of Holy Laughter in Other Religions," quoted in *Spiritual Counterfeit Project Newsletter* (Berkeley, CA) Fall 1994, vol. 19:2, p. 14.

11. A.B. Simpson, "Burn On!" *Hymns of the Christian Life* (Camp Hill, PA: Christian Publications, 1978), #246.

Chapter 10

Leading Personalities

Without a doubt the Toronto Blessing has generated widespread theological controversy. But there is one thing everyone seems to agree upon—the phenomenon at Toronto Airport Christian Fellowship has an uncanny ability to generate headlines and raise eyebrows. Here is just a sampling of what has been said.

A bold declaration at the top of an article by Robert Hough in *Toronto Life* said, "God is alive and well and saving souls on Dixon Road." Below it, a subheading read, "Last January, the Lord descended on the Airport Vineyard church and reduced a roomful of adults into a pack of wild animals. He's been doing encores ever since."[1]

In answering members of Parliament at the British parliamentary prayer breakfast in London in 1995, Rev. W. Harold Fuller, retired SIM missionary executive, stated, "I believe that the Toronto Blessing is from God, and of the world, and of the flesh, and of the devil."[2] This is a rather unique summary from an outstanding Canadian Christian statesman. It seems to say what many people are trying to say. But it also leaves the reader wondering how this can possibly be. A close look at leadership may give us some answers.

The secular Canadian Broadcasting Corporation aired the following on its "Sunday Morning News Hour":

> Planes land every few minutes at Toronto's Pearson Airport, right over the top of Toronto's Vineyard Church. . . . [T]he Toronto branch has such a direct line to the Holy Spirit, some 40,000 people from around the world have flown in to "do carpet time," giggle with "The Holy One," and speak in tongues. Staid and more established churches have been looking on with alarm and jealousy, and if they aren't jazzing up their own services, they are denouncing the airport church as the work of the devil.[3]

There were varying degrees of interpretations of news reports. In June 1994, the *Toronto Globe* reported, "Revival church—people are flocking to join a congregation that breaks into laughter, falls to the ground, and roars like a lion."[4] Chevreau claimed this "put the renewal in a positive light."[5] A Fifth Estate guest calls it "mass hysteria" in the church.[6]

Though the Toronto Blessing is widely purported to be a genuine work of the Holy Spirit, human personalities still figure very prominently in any discussion of this phenomenon. Among those that loom largest is that of John Arnott, senior pastor of the Toronto Airport Christian Fellowship. An understanding of who he is and where he comes from theologically is very important in coming to grips with what is taking place at TACF.

From *Toronto Life* came this description:

> John Arnott, senior pastor of the Airport Vineyard, is about as average looking as you could imagine: fifty-three years old, twenty pounds overweight, a barbershop haircut. When I met with him, his voice was a warm ocean of calm, and I quickly got the impression he wouldn't shout if his pants caught on fire. Yet in the Christian world, this rumpled preacher is now credited with grooming the latest earthly contact point for God's great power.[7]

What happened that such an unassuming man should be honored with so much attention from the media, from both antagonistic and sympathetic churches, and from religious as well as secular publishing companies?

In his book *The Father's Blessing*, John Arnott states that he became a Christian at a Billy Graham rally "about forty years ago."[8] He attended the nondenominational Ontario Bible College from 1966 to 1968. For over ten years he managed a travel agency he opened and traded in real estate.[9] This background gave him the exceptional ability to advertise and accommodate the preparation for the Toronto Blessing.

After a trip to Indonesia in 1981, he started an independent, evangelical church in his wife's home city, Stratford[10]—more famous for the Shakespeare Festival than religion. His church was casual, contemporary and "accepting of the Holy Spirit."[11]

In 1987 the Lord again moved upon John and Carol to move to the Toronto suburb of Etobicoke to start a Vineyard fellowship in his mother's home. He then moved to a small strip mall near the prominent corner of Dixie and Derry Roads in Mississauga. Throughout that time he was dealing with the same frustrations as many of his peers in the Vineyard movement. He wanted healings, and he wanted prophecy, all the while getting burned out and discouraged by the impotence of the church.[12]

Arnott says, "After a while, you start to feel that the devil's too big, and God's too small."[13] In his desperation he looked for something that would stimulate, something that would produce the results he had seen in the ministries of two of his heroes in the faith, Kathryn Kuhlman and Benny Hinn.

Guy Chevreau writes, with John Arnott's blessing, "Back in the late '60s and early '70s,

John was significantly impacted by Kathryn Kuhlman's ministry, and later on, Benny Hinn's, which began in Toronto."[14] (This foundation will be explored in the next chapter.)

"He was deeply impressed with the fruit, the results of these ministries, for he saw hundreds of people receive a powerful, life-transforming touch from the Lord. He went to many of their meetings, and in significant ways they laid an imprint for the future direction and conduct of his ministry."[15]

In September of 1992, John and his wife Carol went to several Toronto meetings conducted by his old friend, Benny Hinn, at Maple Leaf Gardens, home of the Toronto Maple Leafs. They watched with awe at the demonstration of empowerment with authority over people's lives. Out of this, John was persuaded that he could reach Toronto for Christ.[16]

In June of 1993, they went to a Rodney Howard-Browne meeting in Fort Worth, Texas, in conjunction with Kenneth Copeland Ministries. Rodney moved up and down the aisles, shouting into a cordless microphone, "Fill. Fill. Fill" and "Let the bubble activate your belly" and "Go get him, Lord." *Catch the Fire* states, "When all the smoke cleared there was John and one other man still standing" among the 200 pastors who came forward.[17]

The following November John and Carol went to Argentina and met Claudio Freidzon who had come "home powerfully anointed from a Benny

Hinn service." Arnott says, "Carol went flying" as Claudio prayed for her at a conference. John merely went down, not knowing whether he was "to stand, fall, roll or forget it."[18]

There are two things the reader may have detected. John was living in discouragement and desperation. Good decisions may be made in that atmosphere, but it is not a good time to make decisions.

Come with me to a recent Sunday morning service at the Airport church to see what has transpired. The Toronto Blessing had its second anniversary on January 20, 1996.[19] It is no longer part of the official Vineyard movement or denomination,[20] although Vineyard pastors are still being used extensively. The following is a very abbreviated account of my experience.

John and Carol Arnott had just arrived home from ministries in England, but there was not the joy in the service that one might expect for such an occasion. About 650 people gathered in the spacious auditorium—it is not referred to as a sanctuary. As the service was about to start, we were told that the center section was for regular attendees only. A few visitors had to move.

The singing was typically Vineyard in style, but with Arnott and a different music team than the one I mentioned in chapter 8, the service seemed more professional. The method of musical manipulation, described in chapter 5, worked to perfection. The congregation was soon controlled by the musicians and singers, just like at a rock concert, only more subdued. Soon people were energetically participating in the demonstrations. The louder and faster the music, the higher the people "pogoed," the harder they clapped and the greater was the swaying and waving.

Rev. Arnott announced he would read from Romans chapter 6 and opened his Bible while asking the people to do the same. There were very few Bibles evident. Then he called his wife Carol to the platform to testify. The Bible never got read. It was put on the lectern so John and the chairman could hold their hands over Carol "to soak her."[21]

To me, this borders on the occult. There is no scriptural foundation for such methods. It is the practice of the New Age Movement.[22] I have seen elders doing this when they anoint the sick for healing. I immediately caution them. The Bible specifically says to "lay hands on the sick" (Mark 16:18).

It does not say that we are to find the aura. Defensively people say to me, "But we can feel waves coming from the person." And my reply is, "I know you can. I used to do that before I became a Christian. But I left such shamanistic practices behind nearly fifty years ago."

Then down Carol went with a scream. They placed her right in front of the lectern. She continued to writhe for some time with her upper body thrusting up and down. John said, "She just needs a new soaking." Two ladies came to "soak" her, sometimes pumping their hands up and down as though imparting something into her body. Occasionally they would go through the motions of plucking things out of her body and throwing the invisible objects aside. Every once in a while Carol writhed and screamed out.

Two new workers were added to the staff that morning. I anticipated an installation service with the laying on of hands and prayer. In First Timothy 4:13-14, Paul says:

> Give attention to the public reading of Scripture, to exhortation and teaching. Do not neglect the spiritual gift within you, which was bestowed upon you through the prophetic utterance with the laying on of hands by the presbytery.

And again in Second Timothy 1:6, he states, "I remind you to kindle afresh the gift of God which is in you through the laying on of my hands."

Instead John pushed them on the forehead. The new pastor fell to his hands and knees and roared like a lion. His wife was caught by the catchers and laid out to the right of the lectern, where she remained for the entire service. (Cynically I found myself saying, "Two down and one to go. They always have three.")

Then Kelly was called forward to testify. She had been down in Toronto's inner city to work among the destitute, providing food and clothing. I said, "Praise the Lord." But I was the only one to say so. There had been much noise, shouting and laughing when the previous ones were being slain. Now all was quiet. Apparently this menial ministry to the poor wasn't exciting enough to encourage laughter.

Kelly, of course, would be the third model during the preaching time. But she didn't go down. After several attempts, she was taken over to my side of the auditorium and a ministering team worked on her. The chairman for the morning then began to convulse, shook his head vigorously and fell into the arms of two catchers. He was placed to the left of the lectern. Now the scene was set, one on each side and one in the middle.

Kelly was prayed for, counseled and several attempts were made to have her slain. This went on for over fifteen minutes. Finally they gave up. Kelly was in tears. Sadly she walked to her chair near the front. I imagine she felt like a "dud." The other three had helpers "soaking them in the Spirit," but she would have to go about serving Jesus on her own. Her request for helpers, food and clothing got no response. It wasn't something people would shout about. I could not think of any Scriptures to describe the other three. But the Bible came through clear and plain for Kelly:

> I say to you, to the extent that you did
> it to one of these brothers of Mine, even

the least of them, you did it to Me. . . .
To the extent that you did not do it to
one of the least of these, you did not do
it to Me. (Matthew 25:40, 45)

Kelly was fulfilling the commands of Scripture to minister to the poor. I was proud of her. Remember the motto for this great renewal? "That we may walk in God's love and give it away."[23] I wondered how this motto and Kelly's experience fitted together.

Rev. Arnott asked how many read their Bibles regularly. Not more than twenty-five out of 650 raised their hands. He exhorted them to read the Bible "and all that stuff." He picked up the Bible again at Romans 6 and began to preach. The sermon was not great considering it was coming from a man that was now being heralded as "bringing in a new thing,"[24] but I think it was very acceptable for this crowd, which in my estimation appeared spiritually immature.

Regarding the preaching at TACF, others have observed the lack of depth. James A. Beverly says that the meetings tolerate exceedingly weak and at times erroneous biblical exposition, are excessively routinized and fall short of New Testament standards of being conducted decently and in order. He adds that prophecies should be rigorously screened and tendencies toward anti-intellectualism and elitism sould be more firmly resisted.[25]

Arnott referred to Carol on the floor as having been Lutheran, then Vineyard—and now what?

She screamed out, but John ignored her. Her "soakers" shook their heads and began plucking again. It might have done more good if they all had listened to John's sermon.

The new male staff member was now on his stomach, pumping up and down. Soon he and those "soaking" him sat in a circle audibly visiting with one another while John continued to preach. He was now at Romans 6:12-13, 15:

> Do not let sin reign in your mortal body that you should obey its lusts, and do not go on presenting the members of your body to sin as instruments of un-righteousness. . . . Shall we sin because we are not under law but under grace?

Carol shouted, "Yes! Yes!"

The other lady on the floor shouted back, "No! No!"

It was a wake-up call to a drowsy crowd, and there was then much laughter.

John exhorted them to say "no" to sin. Then he "flicked" his body. Many others did the same thing.

"When sex hits your head, get out your Bible. I have to say, 'God help me.' "

The men sitting in the circle all laughed and laughed.

He further exhorted them to put less focus on dealing with the problem and do service. "Ask the Holy Spirit, 'What should I do?' "

Carol shrieked.

The ladies laughed.

John said that they needed more washrooms and more parking spaces. "We need more money."

Carol cried out, "Yes!"

Later Carol shrieked again and John thought that was also a "yes." He said, "Oft times she cries out."

The only verse I could come up with immediately was Luke 9:39—"A spirit seizes him and he suddenly screams, and it throws him into a convulsion, . . . and as it mauls him, it scarcely leaves him." If my diagnosis was right, there should have been a deliverance instead of an encouragment of the spectacle.[26]

At the end of the message, Arnott gave an altar call for people to respond for salvation. Five ladies responded, being brought to the front by their friends. These were all taken to a private place for counseling.

Sinners had been brought in. The Bible had been preached. The Holy Spirit illumined the Word. The unsaved responded. I had to leave the rest in God's hands. I didn't like the service. I didn't like the method. But I also thought of the many who were severely criticizing, who themselves were seeing nothing happen, some of whom had not seen a soul saved in years.

Much time had elapsed, but the service was not over. A brunette came forward and fell backward into the arms of catchers—I did notice that people only fell backward when they felt a catcher's hands on their backs. It was a signal for many others to come forward. Then the brunette got up and immediately began praying for others. Each one fell backward as she prayed for them, unless a catcher was not available. Then they stayed standing and cried.

Rev. Arnott was at work on the opposite side of the auditorium. I needed a closer look at this man in operation. As he prayed for a young lady, she began to fling her arms and head until her entire body was in tumult. Her actions were so frenzied, I wondered if she might injure herself.[27]

Whenever this had happened in my meetings, I would ask the people to step back and pray rather than observe. Sometimes I would segregate the person completely from the group when I thought it was a dangerous situation. Every time, to this date, demons have been cast out in such instances. But here the people gathered around to rejoice that another person was being filled with the Spirit and/or prophesying.

This lady was completely out of control. Even Arnott gave the appearance that he was helpless. After all, did not Airport Christian Fellowship's "Statement of Faith" say in part, "We believe the Holy Spirit lives in our lives as believers and brings . . . self-control into our lives"?

It appeared to me that this whole thing was what Paul talked about in Second Thessalonians 2:11: "And for this reason God will send upon them a deluding influence so that they might believe what is false." If this is the case, what or who would be the deluding influence? It would be trite to simply say it is Satan. We need to know how these delusions take place, and if they do, how we can counteract them.

I had hoped to see Carol Arnott in action, but for the most part, I was disappointed. This time they had her on the floor instead of doing some of the things I had read about.

It has been reported that in earlier meetings she would point her finger at someone across the room. That person would fall down in fits of laughter, then get up and point at somebody else across the room. Then that person would fall and laugh. This has been referred to as "flinging the Spirit." John Arnott has said, "This thing is easily transferred."

It reminded me of accounts in the book, *The Faith Healers of the Philippines*. These seasoned "faith doctors" would stand across the room from a patient and merely point at the area of the patient's tumors. Sometimes they made a circling motion with their fingers. An incision would result. Something would pop out and onto the floor. Then the practitioner would heal up the wound perfectly, without a scar, while still standing as far away as the room would allow.

Thousands of people go to the Philippines to see this and to get healed. Travel agents charter whole flights from many parts of the world. Does this sound familiar? Filipino national pastors and missionaries I have questioned say that it really happens. And it happens by the power of the devil. Christians who have participated become continuous problems.

But I did not see anything like that on this particular day. Carol Arnott was still on the floor, being "plucked" by the ministering team and "soaking in the Spirit."

> Once it was the blessing, Now it is the
>   Lord;
> Once it was the feeling, Now it is His
>   Word;
> Once His gift I wanted, Now the Giver
>   own;
> Once I sought for healing, Now Him-
>   self alone.[28]

Endnotes

1. Robert Hough, *Toronto Life Magazine*, February 1995, p. 20.

2. W. Harold Fuller, "Your Turn," *Christian Week*, 1995.

3. Canadian Broadcasting Corporation, "Sunday Morning News Hour," August 1994, as reported in *No Laughing Matter* (Excelsior Spings, MO: Double Crown Publishing, 1995), p. 87.

4. *Toronto Globe and Mail*, June 20, 1994.

5. Guy Chevreau, *Catch the Fire* (London: Harper-Collins, 1944), p. 37

6. "The Fifth Estate," Canadian Broadcasting Corporation, January 1996, available on video cassette.

7. Hough, p. 21.

8. John Arnott, *The Father's Blessing* (Lake Mary, FL: Creation House, 1995), acknowledgments.

9. Hough, p. 21.

10. Chevreau, p. 21.

11. Hough, p. 21.

12. Ibid.

13. John Arnott as quoted by Robert Hough, p. 21.

14. Chevreau, p. 21

15. Ibid.

16. Ibid., p. 22.

17. Ibid., p. 23.

18. Ibid.

19. Doug Koop in *Christian Week*, February 13, 1996, p. 4.

20. "People & Events," *Charisma*, February 1996, p. 12.

21. Warren Smith, *Holy Laughter or Strong Delusion*, Spiritual Counterfeit Project, Vol. 19:2, p. 3.

22. Albert James Dager, "Toward the New Age," "A Special Report on Holy Laughter," *Media Spotlight*, January 1995, p. 13.

23. John Arnott in *Catch the Fire*, Preface, p. viii.

24. See also John Wimber's statement in "Testing the Fruit of the Vineyard," *Media Spotlight*, January 1995, p. 22, "I'm speaking things into existence that God is telling me to speak, because of the anointing. We're moving into a miracle dimension."

25. Glen G. Scorgie quoting James A. Beverly, "Blessing Debated," *Christian Week*, June 18, 1996, p. 14.

26. See also, Luke 4:33-35, 40-41.

27. See Luke 9:39-42 for a scriptural description of this type of event.

28. A.B. Simpson, "Himself," *Hymns of the Christian Life* (Camp Hill, PA: Christian Publications, 1978), #248.

Chapter 11

The Human Influences

I suppose every Christian worker has had someone special in his/her life who has been an influential factor in the molding of a ministry. I had the privilege of working alongside the late Dr. A.W. Tozer[1] for a number of summers in Bible conference work, he as Bible teacher and I as youth speaker.

But I think the one man that influenced me more than any other was Dr. Nathan Bailey. He would come to our home and talk to my wife Gwen and me for days at a time. One time I told him that he could not possibly have time to spend on us like he did, being a district superintendent and vice-president of one of the world's largest missionary societies.[2] He remarked, "Oh, yes, I have. You two have energy. You are always on the move. I can steer you. I have many pastors who are standing still. I can't steer them. But your sails are ready to catch the breeze."

Tozer and Bailey were men of integrity. The Holy Spirit blew through them to fill my "sails," imparting direction and blessing. The Rev. John Arnott also had his sails up to catch the breeze. Let us take a look at what was blowing into them. Was it the wind of the Holy Spirit? What people were the instruments of the wind that caught his sails? Doubtless there were many, but we will look at three in particular.

Kathryn Kuhlman

Perhaps only older readers will remember much about Kathryn Kuhlman, who significantly impacted John Arnott's life and ministry.[3] She died in 1976 after having open heart surgery in Texas, though not necessarily from the surgery itself. The ministry she founded never recovered after her surgery. It was as though her followers were saying, "Physician, heal yourself" (Luke 4:23). In all fairness, this was not justified since "it is appointed for men to die once and after this comes judgment" (Hebrews 9:27).

When she was a child, her father, Joe Kuhlman, was twice the mayor of Concordia, Missouri.[4] The prestige of this office undoubtedly had an impact on her.

In 1938, she married evangelist Burroughs Waltrip, who had abandoned his wife and family. Six years later, in 1944, Kuhlman divorced him.[5] We are told in God's Word, " 'For I hate divorce,' says the LORD, the God of Israel. . . . So take heed to your spirit, that you do not deal treacherously" (Malachi 2:16).

In her ministry center in Pittsburgh, Pennsylvania, Kuhlman brought into the church what she called "holy laughter." This seemed to be reserved especially for those who went down "under the power."[6] She also referred to it as "laughing in the Spirit" when one "under the power" would become hysterical. Since laughter is contagious it often spread to others.

While she frequently referred to her own "death to self," her wardrobe was lavish. She would sweep out onto the stage in her long, flowing gowns and in a guttural voice would ask the audience, "Have you been waiting for me?" This would immediately bring a rousing response; the audience was like plastic to be molded. Her basement vault that held her valuables[7] seemed evidence enough that she did not heed Christ's instruction, "Do not lay up for yourselves treasures upon earth, where moth and rust destroy, and where thieves break in and steal. . . . For where your treasure is, there will your heart be also" (Matthew 6:19, 21).

By contrast, her staff received notoriously low salaries, perhaps waiting for the day when her estate would be divided. Ultimately they did receive small portions "from her more than $2 million personal estate,"[8] but the bulk went to some friends she had known for less than a year, according to G. Richard Fisher and M. Kurt Goedelman.[9]

Kuhlman's book *I Believe in Miracles* quickly became a best-seller in America. It was also used extensively overseas, especially in Vietnam. In the book she documents eighty-two cases of healings, all of them dramatic, many of them cancer victims.[10]

After investigating these claims, Dr. William A. Nolen published his findings in a book entitled *Healing: A Doctor in Search of a Miracle*. It is his expressed opinion that none of the healings were legitimate.[11] He endeavored to re-examine all eighty-two cases, but some would not cooperate. Others could not be found. Of the twenty-three who did agree to be interviewed, none of the people were healed, although some received temporary relief. Was it all fraud in an effort to build up earthly treasure?

In 1974, I was in Pittsburgh for a church crusade with my own denomination. I thought it was a wonderful opportunity to see Ms. Kuhlman in operation. I asked my host pastor if he would take me to the weekly Thursday afternoon meeting. He replied that he would not and said that I was not welcome to go as long as I was his guest. However, if I wanted to make a buck or two, he suggested somewhat facetiously, I could collect by telling them I was from Canada and suffering from cancer. Kuhlman would call me forward, he said, slay me in the Spirit, heal me and have me testify. I had faith that my fellow worker was giving more than a jaundiced assessment, so I declined the challenge and instead stayed in my room, studied my Bible and prayed for the evening service.

Kathryn Kuhlman is one of the people who became a hero of the faith for John Arnott. Both he and Benny Hinn were strongly impacted by her. Since Hinn also significantly influenced Arnott, perhaps it would provide valuable insights to examine the Kuhlman-Hinn connection.

Benny Hinn

Hinn became so enthralled with Kuhlman that he sang in her choir in order to observe her style. "Her ability to control a group fascinated Hinn. It would appear that her chief ability was whipping a crowd into a frenzie."[12] After her death he visited her grave for inspiration.

In an apparent effort to emulate Kuhlman, Hinn claimed mayoralty connections.[13] According to him, his father Costandi Hinn was the mayor of Jaffa during Benny's childhood.[14] An attempt to verify this claim found no supporting evidence. Jaffa ceased to exist as a separate city by 1948 having irreversibly merged[15] with Tel Aviv to become Tel Aviv-Yafo, the largest city of Israel.[16] All the mayors of the former Jaffa from 1918 to 1948 were Arabs, and no Hinn is mentioned. Benny even says his family was Greek Orthodox[17] which further precludes his father from holding this office.

A list of the mayors for Jaffa and Tel Aviv-Yafo was provided by the Museum of History of Tel Aviv-Yafo. It reads as follows:

Israel Rokach was mayor of Tel Aviv from 1936 to 1950.

Israel Rokach was mayor of Tel Aviv-Yafo from 1950 to 1952.

Chaim Levanon was mayor of Tel Aviv-Yafo from 1952 to 1959.

Mordekhai Namir was mayor of Tel Aviv-Yafo from 1959 to 1969.

Yehoshua Rabinowitz was mayor from 1969 to 1974, and Shlomo Lahat to the present.

It is important for the reader to notice that Benny Hinn's connection to the office of mayor appears to be only a dream. Could it be rooted in his passion to pattern Kathryn Kuhlman more closely?

Inconsistencies also surround his account of religious rites performed after his birth. Born on December 3, 1952, Hinn claims to have been christened by Benedictus, Patriarch of Jerusalem.[18] But Benedictus was not elected to that honor until January 1957, according to *The Jerusalem Post*.[19] Perhaps we can excuse Hinn for these discrepancies due to certain alleged tendencies in Arab culture; in that part of the world, stating a wish as an accomplished fact is reportedly quite common.

Conflicting reports also appear in descriptions of Hinn's conversion. In the *PTL Family Devotional* of January 17, 1981, he wrote, "I got saved in Israel in 1968," just before his family immigrated to Toronto.[20] Next, in a testimony in St. Louis, Missouri, he stated, "Then in 1968, I was only about 13 or 14. . . . Someone witnessed to me and I got saved—right then—which was right after 1968."[21] This was in Toronto.

Then in his book, *Good Morning, Holy Spirit*, he tells of his conversion in 1972, when an angel "dropped me on Don Mills Road—right at the Georges Vanier School and took me inside the room where I was saved."[22]

In his taped account, the story is considerably different. "A school mate, Michelle, took me by the hand and pulled me to the prayer meeting. . . . I get into this room and there's Bob Tadman . . . [and] another called Paul Pynkoski."[23] According to research, "none of these key players mentioned by Hinn remembers the meeting where Hinn says he was converted."[24]

Hinn also tries to document being healed or freed from stuttering. He gives a number of different accounts of this, citing several different cities. Is this fuzzy thinking or a deliberate attempt to mislead? Perhaps only Hinn himself knows the answer. I suppose in all of this, the old saying comes into play: "When you tell the truth, you don't have to remember what you say."

Rev. David Lockwood, who invited Hinn to speak at Shilo Fellowship in Oshawa states, "I can't recall him stuttering."[25] Jim McCalister was co-pastor of The Catacombs which met in downtown Toronto. He says Hinn "spoke very rapidly and he wasn't always with it. Benny was a little bit of a problem to me in terms of exuberance for anything that was a little bit frothy."[26] Further, "We used Benny in a production where he shared the dramatic antiphonal declaration of a psalm which required clear speech and clear rhythm." Both of these events took place before Hinn professes to have been healed, and there was no evidence of stuttering.

Could the reason that Hinn says he was delivered from this impediment of speech be further evidence of patterning Kuhlman? Kathryn reportedly stuttered in a thick southern accent when she was a child and got help through a self-improvement program.[27] If this is the objective, Hinn goes one better and claims to be miraculously healed.

From this brief glimpse into Hinn's background and character, we turn to his theology. Couched on the cushion of orthodoxy are some very amazing, disturbing claims and beliefs.

In his book, *The Anointing*, Hinn states that Christians live at four different levels. The first is being saved. The second is being baptized in the Spirit. Then he goes on to the "higher levels"—the presence and the anointing. According to Hinn, unless Christians achieve these last two, God cannot and will not bless and use them. Hinn says he has reached level four, the anointing, but that very few ever get this far.[28] Consequently, being one of them puts him in an elite category. This is a far cry from "Do nothing from selfishness or empty conceit, but with humility of mind let each of you regard one another as more important than himself" (Philippians 2:3).

He further explains that he first realized he had "the anointing" when he was preaching in Trinity Pentecostal Church in Oshawa, Ontario on December 7, 1974.[29] "I held up my hands to pray and one hundred people present fell on the floor. That's when I became aware of my tremendous power," Hinn wrote.[30] This same date and place was one of several times and locales where he claims to have been delivered from stuttering.[31]

The anointing seems to put Benny Hinn on an equal basis with God. He tells a story of holding hands with the Holy Spirit while he was waiting for a meal in London, England. When his host called him to eat, he asked leave of the Holy Spirit. The Holy Spirit replied that He needed Hinn's fellowship for just five more minutes.[32]

On the doctrine of the Trinity, Hinn also has some unusual teachings. In an October 13, 1990 broadcast, he said:

> God the Father is a person, God the Son is a person, God the Holy Spirit is a person, but each of them is a triune being by Himself. If I can shock you, and maybe I should, there are *nine* of them [italics mine]. God the Father is a person with his own personal spirit, with his own personal soul and his

own personal spirit body. . . . [Each] is
a triune being within Himself. . . . The
Holy Ghost, who is a triune being who
walks in a spirit body and He has hair
. . . has eyes . . . has a mouth . . . has
hands.[33]

Dr. Gary Johnson, professor of Church History at the Philadelphia College of the Bible, responds to Hinn's teaching this way: "He says the Trinity is nine persons and that's heresy. What he's advocating is not a whole lot different than what is advocated by Kenneth Copeland as reported in the book, *Agony of Deceit*."[34] It does sound a little like Mormonism too.

Regarding Jesus, Benny Hinn says there were two deaths on the cross. First, Jesus died spiritually and became one with Satan, thus losing His deity. Next, He died physically, and His human spirit was taken into hell. Then after three days of torment, "Jesus was reborn."[35] In a taped message, Hinn warns us, "Don't question this teaching. Only the immature question it."[36] This is simply a rehash of the teachings of Essek W. Kenyon (1867-1948), in his *New Creation Realities*.[37]

Another remarkable piece of heresy is Hinn's teaching that when a person is born again, that person becomes deity, literally a God-man.

May I [Hinn] say it like this? You are a
little God on earth running around. . . .

Say after me, "Within me is a God-man" . . . Now let's say, "I am a God-man." . . . I am not, hear me, I am not part of Him, I am Him! The Word has become flesh in me! When my hand touches someone, it's the hand of Jesus touching somebody. . . . So I'm Benny Jehovah![38]

This is most amazing. When the Mormons give teaching like the above, evangelicals throw up their hands in holy horror. But when Benny Hinn does the same thing, a host of believers make Hinn a hero for giving us new teaching. Of course, he says, "Only the immature question it."[39] And who wants to be labeled as immature?

What a contrast to Widdington's nineteenth-century hymn to which A.B. Simpson wrote the music:

> Not I but Christ be honored, loved, ex-
> alted;
> Not I but Christ be seen, be known, be
> heard;
> Not I but Christ in every look and action;
> Not I but Christ in every thought and
> word.
>
> Christ, only Christ, no idle word e'er
> falling;
> Christ, only Christ, no needless bus-
> tling sound;

> Christ, only Christ, no self-important
> bearing;
> Christ, only Christ, no trace of "I" be
> found.
>
> Oh, to be saved from myself, dear Lord!
> Oh, to be lost in Thee!
> Oh, that it might be no more I,
> But Christ that lives in me![40]

The whole issue here is the sufficiency of the Holy Scriptures. Hinn appeals his case to knowledge gained through extra-biblical revelation, as does John Arnott, Kathryn Kuhlman and another one of Arnott's "heroes of the faith," Rodney Howard-Browne.

Rodney Howard-Browne

Holy laughter had its contemporary beginnings with evangelist Rodney Howard-Browne. He is an enigma—a baffling, puzzling problem. All who have written about him seem to either love him or hate him.

He was born in Port Elizabeth, South Africa in 1961. He "committed his life to Christ at the age of five and had a formative experience of the Holy Spirit as an eight year old." So states David Roberts, editor of Alpha and author of *The Toronto Blessing*.[41]

Like Wimber and Hinn, he belonged to a music group, thus coming to understand the power of music to control crowd emotions.[42]

Whether this is good or bad depends largely on the motive of the one in charge. It is the old question: Does the end justify the means? And then: Is the end an appropriate end?

Howard-Browne helped pioneer the Johannesburg Rhema Church, a Word of Faith church associated with Kenneth Hagin.[43] He received his Doctor of Ministry degree from the Pentecostal-oriented School of Bible Theology in San Jacinto, California, via the correspondence method. He was ordained by The International Convention of Faith Ministries at the Kenneth Hagin headquarters in Tulsa, Oklahoma.[44]

Early in his ministry he spoke at Oral Roberts University and Rhema Bible College in Tulsa, the latter being the Kenneth Hagin school. It is reported that "over 4,000 waited in line on one occasion to receive prayer."[45] Rodney did not allow "ministry teams" as such. That would mean, if he prayed for twenty seconds for each one, that it would take twenty-four hours to accomplish the task, a full day without food or sleep!

In *Charisma* magazine, publisher Steven Strang counseled,

> I urge Rodney Howard-Browne and others who are seeing similar manifestations to be careful, to test the spirits and to submit to godly counsel in order to keep this new revival balanced . . . lest the laughter take over.[46]

It was while Rodney was in Tulsa that Randy Clark, now on the pastoral staff at Toronto Airport Christian Fellowship, went to the meetings and "got zapped." Clark took "it" (holy laughter) back to his Vineyard church in St. Louis, Missouri. He reported these events to the regional Vineyard meeting at Lake Geneva, Wisconsin, in October 1993. In January 1994, Clark went to the Toronto Airport Vineyard and passed "it" on to the first meeting there.[47] The rest is history and the focal point of many books and numerous articles.

It was at the Fort Worth, Texas meetings that Arnott and Clark came to "understand" the meaning of such Howard-Browne terms[48] as,

> You can get a drink of this too. Don't try to reason it. Out of your belly will flow rivers. Let it bubble your belly. . . . Let the bubble activate your belly. . . . Hit him, Lord. . . . Get 'em, Jesus. . . . You are being lifted higher in the spirit realm.[49]

From the pen of Clifford Hill, London, United Kingdom, we receive some further insights:

> The pastor was struck dumb. Although he tried valiantly to articulate words, he lost the power of speech and then gradually lost the use of his limbs and collapsed in a heap on the floor. He re-

mained there for about half-an-hour before attempting to crawl across the stage on all fours to the great amusement of the audience before collapsing in a heap. . . . I immediately asked myself what kind of spirit would this be that would prevent believers from giving a testimony to glorify the name of Jesus—certainly not the Holy Spirit.

Howard-Browne then began to work the whole audience, rhythmically pacing up and down in front of the stage, using a strange tongue that was never interpreted. This gradually became a mantra which climaxed in a piercing high-pitched sound which he held for a long time. . . . An African pastor and a former missionary both immediately said they recognized this as identical with the voodoo call used by witch doctors in summoning up the demons.

By this time most of the audience were affected with a variety of manifestations such as shouting, screaming, laughing, strange noises, body convulsions, arms and legs flying in all directions and heads rolling—in fact the whole place was bedlam—but above it all it was possible to hear a snatch of one man praying loudly . . . "Father, let your will be done."

Rodney reacted strongly, calling for

the bouncers. He said, "That man over there praying! Tell him to shut up!"

Three burly stewards hurried to do his bidding.

He continued, "You can do anything you like in this meeting: you can shout, scream, laugh, turn cartwheels, anything you like, but I am the one who speaks!"[50]

This is all on video as are many other of Rodney Howard-Browne's antics.

There is a great deal more that could be said about Arnott's three main clergy influences in his ministry. However, this is more than sufficient to show an apparent integrity gap in Arnott's foundation.

By contrast, in all my exploration of the Toronto Blessing I find only a simple mention of Billy Graham in Arnott's youth, at a time when Billy Graham impacted Toronto as no other has, and no mention whatsoever of the late Dr. A.W. Tozer, who pastored the famous Avenue Road Church in Toronto from 1959 to 1963 during Arnott's formative years. In addition, his three years at Ontario Bible College, 1966 to 1968, are compressed into a mere sentence. No mention is made at all about the Billy Graham Crusade of May 1995, held in the world-famous Toronto Skydome. God was mightily at work in the whole area, while the then-called Toronto Airport Vineyard Christian Fellowship was endeavoring to work up a revival.

In addition, two of the better-known Christian statesmen in the world and one of the leading Bible colleges in Canada are virtually ignored in the light of unusual manifestations through other people. Arnott says, "We have endeavoured to shift the focus off them" (the manifestations).[51] But the truth comes through loud and clear. In the pro-Toronto Blessing writings, in the anti-Toronto Blessing writings and from my own personal on-the-spot witness of events, the emphasis has been and continues to be on unusual non-biblical manifestations.

However, not all who attended the TACF have been able to accept their teaching. Among those who have left is a group known as the Christian Evangelism Fellowship (CEF). On March 20, 1995, the directors of CEF, Toronto, in a letter addressed to *Faith Today*, and now circulated in printed form, stated their reasons for leaving John Arnott's church as follows:

1. Extra-Biblical teaching on prayer and prophecy with strong "New Age" overtones
2. "Home Bible studies" that were group therapy sessions where Bible study was completely absent
3. A preaching ministry in which the Word of God was handled in a rudimentary way, without the scope and

breadth of a full acquaintance with Scriptures

4. Association with the ministry of Benny Hinn.[52]

In the next chapter we will investigate the underlying roots with an overall view of what has been erroneously described as the Fire of God sweeping across Canada and Europe.

> Once 'twas painful trying,
> Now 'tis perfect trust;
> Once a half salvation,
> Now the uttermost!
> Once 'twas ceaseless holding,
> Now He holds me fast;
> Once 'twas constant drifting,
> Now my anchor's cast.[53]

Endnotes

1. For more information on Tozer, see James L. Snyder, *In Pursuit of God: The Life of A.W. Tozer* (Camp Hill, PA: Christian Publications, 1991).

2. From 1946 to 1960 Nathan Bailey was a district superintendent and from 1960 to 1978 president of The Christian and Missionary Alliance, as recorded in *All for Jesus* (Camp Hill, PA: Christian Publications, 1986), pp. 218, 226f and 239. He was also on the board of the National Association of Evangelicals and the World Relief Commission.

3. Guy Chevreau, *Catch the Fire* (London: Harper-Collins, 1994), p. 21.

4. Kathryn Kuhlman, *I Believe in Miracles* (New York: Pyramid Books, 1969), p. 11.

5. Jamie Buckingham, *Daughter of Destiny* (Plainfield, NJ: Logos International, 1976), pp. 76-78.

6. Benny Hinn, *The Anointing* (Nashville, TN: Thomas Nelson, 1992), p. 86.

7. Buckingham, pp. 2-3.

8. Ibid., pp. 149-153.

9. G. Richard Fisher and M. Kurt Goedelman, *The Confusing World of Benny Hinn* (St. Louis, MO: Personal Freedom Outreach, 1995), pp. 26-32.

10. See Kuhlman, *I Believe in Miracles*. By my count, there are eighty-two healings cited in her book.

11. William A. Nolen, *Healing: A Doctor in Search of a Miracle* (New York: Fawcett, 1974).

12. Fisher and Goedelman, p. 27.

13. Benny Hinn, *Good Morning, Holy Spirit* (Nashville, TN: Thomas Nelson, 1990), p. 18.

14. Hinn, *The Anointing*, p. 21.

15. A. Lewensohn, *Massada Guide to Israel* (Israel: Massada Limited Publishers, 1985), p. 480ff.

16. Alexander Melamid, "Tel Aviv-Yafo," *The World Book Encyclopedia* (Chicago, IL: Field Enterprises Ecucational Corporation, 1973), Vol. 11, p. 19 and Vol. 19, p. 73.

17. Fisher and Goedelman, p. 34.

18. Hinn, *Good Morning, Holy Spirit*, p. 18.

19. *The Jerusalem Post*, December 11, 1980 states January 1957. James Hoade in *Guide to the Holy Land*, p. 89, says 1958.

20. *PTL Family Devotional* (printed by the PTL Network, 1981) for January 17, 1982.

21. Hinn, *The Anointing*, p. 34.

22. Hinn, *Good Morning, Holy Spirit*, pp. 44-46.

23. Ibid., p. 29.

24. Hinn, personal testimony, Orlando Christian Center, July, 1987, cassette tape AO71987.

25. Fisher and Goedelman, p. 48.

26. Ibid., p. 48.

27. Ibid., p. 49.

28. Ibid., p. 21.

29. Hinn, *Good Morning, Holy Spirit*, pp. 44-46.

30. Ibid.

31. Ibid., p. 5.

32. Ibid.

33. Hinn, Orlando Christian Center Broadcast, October 13, 1990.

34. As reported by Bill Alnor and released to the media, October 15, 1990.

35. Stephen F. Cannon, *Benny Hinn and Revelation Knowledge* (St. Louis, MO: Personal Freedom Outreach, 1995), pp. 8-9.

36. Hinn, *Our Position in Christ*, 1988 audio cassette, six tape series.

37. Essek W. Kenyon, *New Creation Realities* (Lynwood, WA: Kenyon's Gospel Publishing Society, 1945), p. 129.

38. Hinn, Spiritual Warfare seminar, Jubilee Christian Center, San Jose, Calif., May 2, 1990.

39. Hinn, *Our Position in Christ*.

40. A.B. Simpson, "Not I, But Christ," *Hymns of the Christian Life* (Camp Hill, PA: Christian Publications, 1978), #264.

41. Dave Roberts, *The Toronto Blessing* (Eastbourne, East Sussex, UK: Kingsway Publications, 1994), p. 83.

42. Ibid., p. 84.

43. Albert James Dager, "Holy Laughter," *Media Spotlight*, January 1995, p. 2.

44. Dave Roberts, pp. 84-86.

45. Ibid., p. 90.

46. As quoted by Dave Roberts in *The Toronto Blessing*, p. 91.

47. Chevreau, *Catch the Fire*, p. 24.

48. Ibid., p. 27.

49. Alan Morrison, *Another Gospel*, video cassette. See also chapter 16, "In the Vernacular."

50. Clifford Hill, *Bringing the Unchanging Word of God to a Changing World* (Nasmith House, London, UK: public letter), November 28, 1994.

51. Chevreau, p. viii.

52. An open letter from Steve and Cheryl Thomson, directors of the Christian Evangelical Fellowship, Toronto, Ontario.

53. A.B. Simpson, "Himself," *Hymns of the Christian Life* (Camp Hill, PA: Christian Publications, 1978), #248.

Chapter 12

Theological Roots

What grows above ground has a direct relationship to the root that grows below. To better understand the strange phenomena that are happening at the Toronto Blessing, it is of vital importance to look at the roots from which they have grown. To do this I have put together a chart. It does not originate with me, but I do not know to whom credit should be given. I have seen similar charts, some more simplified,[1] some more complicated, but all very revealing. Solomon's teaching is indeed apropos:

> That which has been is that which will be, and that which has been done is that which will be done. So, there is nothing new under the sun. Is there anything of which one might say, "See this, it is new"? Already it has existed for ages which were before us. (Ecclesiastes 1:9-10)

The chart is obviously an overview. I have eliminated much in the interest of simplicity, although the subject itself is quite complicated. Some may wish to explore further and supply other headings and data to flesh out the chart for lecture purposes.

Almost any academic will call this chapter overly simplistic and may want to dismiss it. The average reader will find it quite complicated and may need to go through it a number of times to understand the pattern. I have endeavored to make it acceptable to both.

Following the chart (on the next page), I have given brief explanations of what the names and "isms" mean in the breakdown. This way, having seen the theological tree, the reader is able to explore the contents as he or she desires.

In commenting on the main influences in the chart, it may appear to some that I am have left too much to conjecture. But I am merely taking out of each area of philosophy the route that has been taken, either consciously or unconsciously, to arrive at the point at which the Airport Church finds itself today. To some extent the church at large is also affected by these subversive influences.

In my discussion of personalities, and I will discuss some of them again, I do not want to infer that what I write is the essence of that personage. The complexities of the human personality cannot be captured in a few short lines. What I am trying to do, however, is to present those human elements

The Genealogy of a Belief

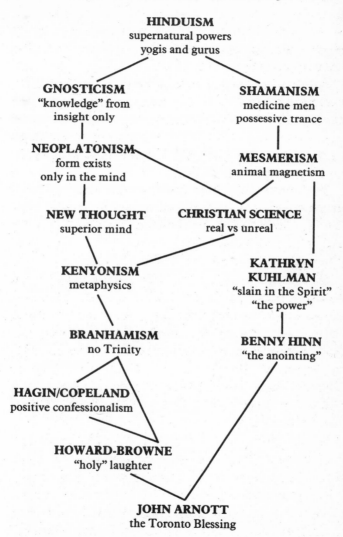

HINDUISM
supernatural powers
yogis and gurus

GNOSTICISM
"knowledge" from
insight only

SHAMANISM
medicine men
possessive trance

NEOPLATONISM
form exists
only in the mind

MESMERISM
animal magnetism

NEW THOUGHT
superior mind

CHRISTIAN SCIENCE
real vs unreal

KENYONISM
metaphysics

KATHRYN
KUHLMAN
"slain in the Spirit"
"the power"

BRANHAMISM
no Trinity

BENNY HINN
"the anointing"

HAGIN/COPELAND
positive confessionalism

HOWARD-BROWNE
"holy" laughter

JOHN ARNOTT
the Toronto Blessing

that have direct bearing on the Toronto Blessing. Some of the people mentioned have done a great work for the Lord. Some of them were led astray through lack of scriptural knowledge. As much as lies within me, my desire is to stick to facts and distance myself from judgment. I was once asked what I thought of a certain man who seemingly had been greatly used of the Lord. I responded, "He has already accomplished more than I ever will. However, I pray that I may never do as much harm as he is now doing!"

Hinduism

Hinduism was the major force to confront the Apostle Thomas when he arrived in India about AD 68, according to the Eastern Orthodox Church. The caste system determines the occupation and almost the total way of life for the Hindu. It is a polytheistic religion with the belief that many divinities make up Brahman. The three most important ones are Brahma, the creator of the universe; Vishnu, its preserver; and Shiva, its destroyer.[2]

There are many Hindu schools of thought or philosophy. "Nyaya" deals with logic. "Vaisheska" deals with the nature of the world. The "Sankhya" school deals with the many theories of creation. "Yoga" is a set of mental and physical exercises so the soul can be relieved of the confinement of the body.[3]

From these few brief statements, it is easy to

see how this "oldest of religions"[4] has been able to infiltrate many foundational beliefs, both false and true. For example, the gnostics mixed Hindu spirituality with knowledge to create a spiritual knowledge not grounded in fact.[5]

But what about the church? Surely it has not been impacted. A close examination raises both questions and eyebrows. Is there now a caste system in the church with varying levels of spiritual attainment? Is this what Hinn is purporting? At the bottom are those who are merely saved. Above them are those who are both saved and baptized by the Spirit. On another step up are those slain-in-the-Spirit people who know "the presence." And at the top are "the presence" people who have also reached "the anointing." (These concepts were discussed more fully in chapter 11 where Benny Hinn appears to put himself on the same level as God.[6])

The power inherent in Hinduism is attested by former Muktananda follower Joy Smith, who was delivered from its influence. According to her:

Swami Baba Muktananda could transfer what was called "guru grace" to his followers through Skaktipat (physical touch). This "grace" triggered the gradual awakening of the Kundali, which in turn produced various physical and emotional manifestations. Manifestations included uncontrollable laughter, roaring, barking, hissing, crying, shaking, etc. Some devotees became mute or unconcious. Many felt themeselves being infused with feelings of great joy, peace and love. At other times the "fire" of Kundali was so overpowering that [his followers] would find themselves involuntarily hyperventilating to cool themselves down.[7]

Gnosticism

Gnosticism developed early in what is often referred to as "the church age." Gnostics held to the theory that knowledge, rather than faith, held the key to the mysteries of life. This knowledge did not come from scientific study, but from spiritual insight.

Endeavoring to harmonize Hindu and Greek philosophy with Christian beliefs and the Bible caused a great deal of grief in the first centuries of Christianity. Setting aside actual fact for the ethereal paved the way for philosophy to infiltrate the church.[8] This led to the age of Neoplatonism.

Neoplatonism

Neoplatonism developed from the philosophy of Plato. It was thought that we are so wholly unreal, that only forms exist, and these forms exist in a place or divine mind beyond the heavens, where our souls can travel when they leave our bodies to fellowship with "the One" that emanates. Impure souls seek permanent satisfaction, which attachment to their bodies prevents them from finding. The realms of bodies and matter are the lowest order. The world of souls is the next up. Then we rise to ideas, which are divine reason and are the brightest realm of emanation.

Neoplatonism was such an important philosophical movement that it influenced St. Augustine (354-430 AD) in developing his principles of Christian theology.[9] "His *City of God* is, in part, a defense of Christianity and the Catholic church," according to Fulton J. Sheen.[10] Once solidly rejected by the evangelical church, Catholicism, especially if it is charismatic, is being embraced by some evangelicals who appear to quote Augustine on an equal basis with God's Word.

At this point, the philosophy of man became a substitute for God's Word and paved the way for New Thought and the New Age Movement.

New Thought

New Thought is the idea that the mind is superior to all material conditions and circumstances. It was advanced in the 1800s by Ralph Waldo Emerson (1803-1882) and was revised at the beginning of the twentieth century.[11] It isn't exactly New Age, but there are parallels. The Gofs, in their book, *The Stormy Search for the Self*, describe an awakening energy that can be triggered by an advanced teacher, yogi or guru. "[There is] a powerful energy source lying dormant in the form of a coiled serpent at the base of the human spine."[12] When freed, it reputedly has the capacity to effect great physical and spiritual healings. This is called "Kundalini."

> Individuals in this process might find it difficult to control their behavior during powerful rushes of this [Kundalini] energy. They often emit various involuntary sounds, and their bodies move in strange and unexpected patterns . . . unmotivated and unnatural laughter or crying, talking tongues . . . and initiating a variety of animal sounds and movements. . . . [T]his process, although sometimes very intense and shattering, is essentially healing.[13]

An observation of Rodney Howard-Browne live or on video reveals that he often touches the forehead and the base of the spine simultaneously. This "double touch" produces the above effects almost every time.[14]

Kenyonism

Essek W. Kenyon (1867-1948)[15] held that Jesus died both physically and spiritually. Thus Jesus needed to be reborn like the rest of us, according to Kenyon. He taught that when Jesus cried, "It is finished,"[16] He was merely referring to the Abrahamic Covenant. *The Dictionary of Pentecostal and Charismatic Movements* states, "Kenyon's writings also became a survival kit for the ministries of Kenneth Hagin and Kenneth Copeland" and had a great influence on T.L. Osborn and Jimmy Swaggert.[17]

Kenyon was a proponent of metaphysics, trying to discover whether things are arranged in some hierarchy or ascending order. Proponents of this teaching then try to discover the top or apex of that hierarchy and how things descend to various levels.[18]

Kenyon was also a proponent of the blood/magic idea.[19] One could speak, apply and plead the blood to keep the death angel away from cattle and dogs, prevent the entrance of germs, stop impending car accidents, repair broken car engines and get us bonuses after receiving our paychecks.[20] And I say, "Presto! Immediate Utopia! Health and wealth to all!"

The hymn, "There Is Power in the Blood," and other similar hymns ring true. But it is not magic. "But if we walk in the light as He Himself is in the light, we have fellowship with one another, and the blood of Jesus His Son cleanses us from all sin" (1 John 1:7). The blood was for atonement, not for fixing broken chariot wheels. Nor did Paul call upon this type of magic to deliver him from assassins—it took 200 soldiers, 70 horsemen and 200 spearmen, according to Acts 23:23.

Branhamism

William Marrion Branham (1909-1965) professed to have received divine visitations at ages three and seven. He taught that believers who had been baptized in the name of the Father and the Son and the Holy Spirit had to be re-baptized in the name of Jesus only in order to be truly saved.[21]

Referring to the seed of the serpent, he says that Eve had sexual intercourse with Satan, and all her descendants go to hell, which to him is non-eternal. The seed of God are all those who receive Branham's teaching. The residue of people must all go through the Great Tribulation. But Branham himself, "having been virgin-born," will be resurrected according to many of his continuing followers.[22]

He claimed to be "the angel of the church in Laodicea" (Revelation 3:14), and that denominationalism was the mark of the beast. He prophesied that by 1977 all denominations would belong to the World Council of Churches under control of the Roman Catholic Church; that the rapture would immediately take place; and that the world would be destroyed. Hagin and Copeland identify him as a prophet.[23] In light of the above, we certainly would have to add the word "false."

Hagin and Copeland

In my opinion, Hagin and Copeland can be

discussed jointly because they are both proponents of the "positive confession" of Kenyon and Branham, who in turn picked it up through Phineas P. Quimby. (See "Christian Science" below for more on Quimby.) Hagin and Copeland are currently on the scene and still espouse this new view of God, namely: "We bring into being what we state with our mouths, since faith is a confession."[24] It is the "name it and claim it" doctrine which was made popular through Jimmy Bakker and the PTL club. It is also called the "health and wealth" doctrine for which there is no biblical basis.

Alan Morrison in his video, *Another Gospel*, states that Hagin and Copeland are "two of the most notorious and dangerous cultists ever to populate the church of Christ."[25] This likely is an overstatement, and to be fair, Chevreau does not mention them in *Catch the Fire*, nor did he put their books in his bibliography. Nevertheless both men have had a great impact on the present situation, as well as the personnel, in what is called the Toronto Blessing.

Shamanism

Now we go to the top right of "The Genealogy of a Belief" and face Shamanism. "Shaman" is a Mongolian word for a priest or medicine man with the capability of casting out demons and bringing blessing. They may use music, dancing, feasts or chants in order to reach the spirit world.[26] The individual actually comes under the control of the shaman, the same as what happens when a person comes under the power of a Hindu guru.[27]

I know of a man who actually thinks he is a dog. He follows his shaman as a dog follows its master. He curls up on the foot of her bed and sleeps when she goes to bed. When she eats, he wants a dish on the floor beside her chair. When he is alone, he acts like an ordinary man and can work at a job. But when with his shaman, she has control.

In 1981 on an Indian reservation I was once asked if I would like to visit the "old man." When I replied that I should be very happy to do so, they said, "Then you don't know what the 'old man' means." But I did, and we went. I was able to lead him to repent and receive Christ. His wife made the same decision. My interpreter-pastor friend asked later, "Do you think they understood what they did?" I could only reply that I did the best I could for these people who were living on twenty years of borrowed time.

Two years later I returned to the reservation just a day before the funeral of this "old woman." When we arrived at the house I said to my friend, "You will have to introduce me. He won't remember me." But the old man called out, "That's Kuglin. Bring him to me. If it wasn't for Kuglin my wife would be in hell today." He had understood. He was no longer a shaman. One cannot be a shaman and a Christian at the same time.

In 1992, a church elder in Lapuyan, Philippines, claimed that he had found a system that really worked. Before praying for someone that was sick, he would go first to the medicine man (shaman). Then whenever he assisted in the anointing and praying for the sick, the sick person would be healed of the present illness. But almost always the person would become afflicted with palsy, the same disease the elder had. This was verified by the pastor. Knowing this, I refused to allow the elder to assist until he was personally delivered. When he repudiated all past evil relationships, he was set free and the transference stopped.

Out of the mental environment of shamanism came a man who "perfected the practice," as we see next.

Mesmerism

Friedrich Anton Mesmer (1734-1815) was an Austrian doctor who pioneered in hypnotism. His theory of "animal magnetism" became known by the term I have signified. He believed that a mysterious fluid flowed through our bodies, and this fluid allowed one person to have a magnetic influence over another person. He went to Paris, France to practice his sessions or seances in which he magnetized patients.[28]

He was considered the faith healer of the eighteenth century. He would walk among his people in pale velvet robes, waving a wand over them. (They didn't have cordless mikes in those days.) Some people felt nothing. Others felt pain. Some felt insects crawling over them. Some had convulsions, sieges of hiccups and laughter. Some went into raving delirium, acting like animals, which was called "the crisis." In effect it was similar to shamanism inasmuch as he became a purveyor of power. When people fell under the power, it was originally called "temple sleep."[29] (Note the similarity to Kathryn Kuhlman's style, which many say she adopted from Mesmer.) Since Freud's first studies were made on hypnotized persons, modern day psychology can actually be traced back at least as far as Mesmer.[30]

Christian Science

It is a little difficult to fit Christian Science into the chart because it has cause and effect on both sides of the chart. Yet it is not central. Mary Baker Eddy (1821-1910) is heralded as the founder.[31] The encyclopedia says in 1866 she suffered a severe head injury and was healed while reading Matthew 9:1-8.[32] However, Burgess and McGee state that Phineas P. Quimby (1802-1866) healed her in 1862.[33]

Quimby preached "the power of the tongue," which resulted in the doctrine of the "positive confession." This in turn guaranteed healing, health, prosperity, wealth and happiness. He is considered to be the founder of New Thought

Theology, a mixture of spiritism, occultism, hypnosis and other aspects of parapsychology.[34]

J.H. Wiggins, one of Mary Baker Eddy's original editors, described Christian Science as "an ignorant revival of one form of ancient gnosticism. It shares the pantheism of Theosophy and Buddhism while employing the terminology of Christianity."[35]

Pandita Ramabai, of the famous Ramabai Mukti Mission, stated that Christian Science was the same philosophy taught in India for over 4,000 years that had wrecked millions of lives. "It is a philosophy of nothingness," she said.[36]

J. Oswald Sanders writes that it was Quimby, not Eddy, who founded and named Christian Science.[37] If this is so, Quimby is guilty of developing two very diabolical systems.

A discussion of the beliefs of Kathryn Kuhlman, Benny Hinn and Rodney Howard-Browne are included in chapter 11. For comments on John Arnott, see chapter 10. It doesn't take any imagination to see where these four people picked up their philosophies. I call them philosophies because much of their belief systems are not based on the Scriptures.

Look again now at the chart and you will see the logical evolution of beliefs that go back to Hinduism, but take two different courses, ultimately blending together into what has been described as the Toronto Blessing. By reading books issued by personnel of the Toronto Airport Christian Fellowship, we are able to point back to the influence of current prophets, who in turn can be traced back, back and back.

> Once 'twas busy planning,
> Now 'tis trustful prayer;
>> Once 'twas anxious caring,
>> Now He has the care;
> Once 'twas what I wanted,
> Now what Jesus says;
>> Once 'twas constant asking,
>> Now 'tis ceaseless praise.[38]

Endnotes

1. Alan Morrison, "How the Holy Spirit Came to Town," *Evangelical Times*, November, 1994, p. 17.

2. Ione Lowman, *Non-Christian Religions* (Wheaton, IL: Van Kampen Press, n.d.), p. 46.

3. Charles S. White, "Hinduism," *The World Book Encyclopedia* (Chicago, IL: Field Enterprises Educational Corporation, 1973), Vol. 9, pp. 224-225.

4. Ibid.

5. Ibid.

6. Benny Hinn, *The Anointing* (Nashville, TN: Thomas Nelson Publishers, 1992), pp. 170ff.

7. "Some Examples of Holy Laughter in Other Religions," *Spiritual Counterfeits Project*, Fall 1994 Newsletter, 19:2, p. 14.

8. Albert E. Avey, "Gnosticism," *The World Book Encyclopedia*, Vol. 8, p. 228.

9. Robert Brumbaugh, "Neoplatonism," *The World Book Encyclopedia*, Vol. 14, p. 117.

10. Fulton J. Sheen, "Augustine," *The World Book Encyclopedia*, Vol. 1, p. 864.

11. John Clendenning, "New Thought," *The World Book Encyclopedia*, Vol. 14, p. 236.

12. "Some Examples of Holy Laughter in Other Religions," *Spiritual Counterfeit Project*, Fall 1994 Newsletter, 19:2, p. 14.

13. Ibid.

14. Alan Morrison, *Another Gospel* (video cassette of Rodney Howard-Browne and Kenneth Copeland) Diakrisis Publications, London, England.

15. S.M. Burgess and G.M. McGee, eds., *Dictionary of Pentecostal and Charismatic Movements* (Grand Rapids, MI: Zondervan, 1988), p. 517.

16. Essek W. Kenyon, *New Creation Realities* (Lynwood, WA: Kenyon's Gospel Publishing Society, 1945), p. 131.

17. Burgess and McGee, p. 517.

18. Louis O. Kattsoff, "Metaphysics," *The World Book Encyclopedia*, Vol. 13, p. 354.

19. Kenyon, pp. 44f.

20. H.A. Maxwell Whyte, *The Power of the Blood*, (Springdale, PA: Witaker House, 1973), pp. 18, 39-40, 53-54, 64, 87.

21. Burgess and McGee, pp. 95-96.

22. Ibid.

23. Ibid.

24. Ibid.

25. Morrison, *Another Gospel*.

26. "Shamans," *The World Book Encyclopedia*, Vol. 17, p. 297.

27. Mervyn S. Garnarino, "American Indians (Shamans)," *The World Book Enclyclopedia,* Vol. 10, p. 122.

28. George Rosen, "Mesmer, Franz," *The World Book Encyclopedia,* Vol. 13, p. 345.

29. Morrison, *Another Gospel.*

30. Harold Rosen, "Hypnotism," *The World Book Encyclopedia,* Vol. 9, p. 428.

31. "A Critical Review by the Christian Scientists," *The World Book Enclyclopedia,* Vol. 3, p. 406.

32. William B. Davis, "Eddy, Mary Baker," *The World Book Encyclopedia,* Vol. 6, p. 47.

33. Burgess and McGee.

34. Ibid.

35. J. Oswald Chambers, *Heresies and Cults* (London: Lakeland, 1971), p. 43.

36. Ibid.

37. Ibid., pp. 43-44.

38. A.B. Simpson, "Himself," *Hymns of the Christian Life* (Camp Hill, PA: Christian Publications, 1978), #248.

Chapter 13

Those Spectacular Healings

"**D**avid Stark" and "miracle" are words tied closely together whenever healing and the Toronto Airport Christian Fellowship are discussed. I knew this, but I wondered what actually happened. Was he really healed? What documentation was there? Was there any medical verification? This is what I discovered, and it is couched in controversy.

Much has been made of the miraculous healing of David Stark's cancer at the Toronto Blessing meeting held December 15, 1994 at 3:40 p.m. He testified of this during the following evening service.[1] There was no medical confirmation of the healing between the afternoon and evening meetings.

From that time until now there has been much controversy. Some Baptists have risen up in "holy horror." They contend that since divine healing is not for us today, this healing, if there was one, must not be from God. This is further fueled, of course, by the Canadian Broadcasting

Corporation's report on "The Fifth Estate," that David Stark ushers at a Baptist church in Seattle where Rev. Wendell Smith is the pastor.[2] At the opposite end of the continuum are those in the charismatic camps who simply say, "Hallelujah" and keep on praising God.

While "The Fifth Estate" did a remarkable job of reporting, there was obviously difficulty in editing a six-hour film into a few minutes of program, which resulted in some incorrect statements, which I learned after interviewing Stark himself. For instance, Stark and Smith minister with Cities Ministries, an independent group affiliated with the Pastors and Ministers Association of the greater Seattle area, not in a Baptist church.

I Believe in Divine Healing

On Friday, March 15, 1996 I spoke with David Stark to hear his story firsthand. But before I share what I learned, I want to give a personal word of testimony. I believe as the Bible states, "Jesus Christ is the same yesterday and today, yes and forever" (Hebrews 13:8), and from personal experience I know divine healing is real.

In July of 1966, my doctors confirmed that I was totally and permanently disabled. I therefore qualified for a total disability pension from the Canadian government. However, I refused to sign the papers to receive this pension because I believed Jesus was healing me. Not that I would be healed some time in the future, but that I was in the process of being healed right then. I based this on Scripture and on the fact that I had had the elders of the Owen Sound Alliance Church anoint and pray for me accordingly.

Through the years 1965 to 1967, I was hospitalized ten times for extended periods in Ottawa, Owen Sound and London, Ontario. My condition had deteriorated from aggravating pain during my third pastorate to total disability in my fourth pastorate while ministering in our nation's capital, Ottawa.

By the beginning of 1967, I was so crippled that my right shoulder was directly above my left hip. My left leg had shrunk two-and-one-half inches in length. My previously muscular legs, that in my youth had propelled me into a track and field star, had wasted away from eighteen inches at the calf to a mere eight inches. My upper chest stuck out. My head was lopsided. I had excruciating headaches and temporary blind spells. There was also sarcoidosis of the lungs. I had lost the proper use of my legs and partial use of my arms. My right leg dragged and sometimes would not work at all.

While there were many helpful people, both Christian and non-Christian, who graciously provided much positive assistance, there were also those who extended non-scriptural and non-professional help.

"Your problem is the result of sin. Just confess your sin and God will heal you."

"It is obvious that you have demons."

"Don't be foolish. Healing isn't for us today."

On and on it went. I had to remind myself that the devil is the master accuser.

I did receive medical help to get my legs working again while in the Civic Hospital in Ottawa in June of 1967. I never have had any assistance for my arms, other than God's miraculous intervention. All four limbs now work perfectly. But following surgery my back became more twisted and my left leg thinner. Although I have nothing to base this on, I think if I had been content with the original miracle I would still be all bent up.

The doctors said that the further twisting of my body was the result of the operation. But I believed Jesus, the Great Physician, could do better, and our family kept trusting God for a full recovery. The day came when I could throw away my built-up shoe. My body gradually straightened. My chest went back into place. My head returned to normal. No more headaches or blind spells. Sometime between checkups for sarcoidosis, it disappeared completely without medication, while I was in the hospital—a miracle, plus eleven months of ongoing divine healing. I have had no pain or disability since and it has been almost thirty years.

But Job's comforters were still there.

"You know Satan can heal too."

"Well, we will see how long this lasts."

But after so many years, Satan attacks in a different way. Now there are those who say, "I just can't believe it." Some day I will die, and there will be some who will exclaim, "I knew it wouldn't last."

David Stark: The Latest Word

Now here is the story of David Stark. His cancer had been definitely confirmed by his Washington state physician, Dr. Kyle Bryan.[3] David sought prayer from his local church body in Bellevue, part of the greater Seattle area. His pastor directed him to travel to the Toronto Blessing and he would be healed there.[4]

Personally I am opposed to this type of maneuvering. God is also in Bellevue. If a person has to travel thousands of miles to get healed, then God has limited Himself to healing only the ones who have sufficient funds to travel. Further, the Bible says, "Is anyone among you sick? Let him call for the elders of the church, and let them pray over him, anointing him with oil in the name of the Lord; and the prayer offered in faith will restore the one who is sick" (James 5:14-15).

There are a few problems with this today because we have drifted so far from the Scriptures. Some churches do not have elders, either elected or appointed, since one of the fads of the day is "going it alone." Other churches have elders who are almost completely lacking in faith. They have not seen God do anything in years. In some situations, in an effort to "be organized" churches have elected elders who have neither faith nor wisdom as required by the first lay elections in Acts 6:1-5.

David took the advice of his pastor and traveled the 2,500 miles to Toronto. He, like I had been years earlier, was desperate for a touch from God. And God did seem to be working in Toronto. David was taking "up to fifteen shots of morphine a day" to assuage the pain. On the phone, he told me it was eighteen shots, so the announcement in Toronto was not overstated. In the Airport Vineyard newsletter it was stated that the "doctors estimated his life span in hours as cancer consumed his body."[5]

During the afternoon meeting of December 15, 1994, David suddenly felt a fire go through his body and all pain ceased. At the first anniversary service of the Toronto Blessing, January 20, 1995, John Arnott announced that David Stark had been healed. This was on the strength of a letter from Dr. Kyle Bryan that stated that David's clinical response following the prayer meeting in Toronto was nothing short of miraculous.

Dr. Bryan also made it clear that full medical testing had not been completed on David since his return from Toronto. However, blood tests had shown good functioning of David's bone marrow and that his overall status had dramatically improved. What particularly impressed Dr. Bryan was the change in David's pain level. And it was the release of pain about which David had testified.[6] Was this sufficient to report to a "massive congregation" that David had been healed? It would be a pretty dead pastor who wouldn't, in my estimation. When I was privileged to see a blind person healed in the Philippines, I immediately reported it to my prayer supporters.

In February 1995, it was revealed through Medical Renaissance Imaging that David's cancer was growing. However, David had experienced tremendous relief from pain.[7] On the Canadian television program, "The Fifth Estate," available now on video cassette, we were all able to see David, his wife, pastor and doctor.

In my conversation with him, exactly fifteen months after the original healing, David told me, "When I was discharged from the army I weighed 185 pounds. With my cancer I went down to 111 pounds. Now I am back up to 145 pounds! Praise the Lord!"[8] And I praised the Lord with him. Perhaps if we all praised the Lord instead of criticizing this act, the devil wouldn't have so much space to maneuver.

David also told me that he had had a tumor on his head. This was gone and there was no trace of it. He experienced a miracle in the elimination of pain. Now he is in the process of divine healing.[9] I look forward to the day when he, like myself, can enjoy divine health. While he is able to carry a full work load of ministry through his church, he does have attacks of pain at times from spinal cord compression. Laying aside all theological prejudices, David is worthy of our prayers.

No doubt Stark will experience in the 1990s what I experienced in the 1960s—a mixture of skepticism and praises. And someday he, like myself, will die. Then some people will say, "I knew it wouldn't last!"

There are many misconceptions about divine healing. In our modern age, some say it is synonymous with medical healing. But this would suggest that no healing took place between the time of Jesus and today. This cannot be because the Bible must be valid any place in the world at any time. Others incorrectly link divine healing to metaphysical healing or mind cure, magnetic healing or spiritism. Divine healing is not prayer cure nor will power. And certainly it is not defiance of God's will.[10] Since the Bible says we will all die, then it cannot be physical immortality. Nor is it healing for hire because all God's gifts are free.[11] In my opinion, a wise believer will flee from the mercenary healers of our day.

As A.B. Simpson put it a century ago, "It is the supernatural Divine power of God infused into human bodies, renewing their strength and replacing the weakness of the suffering human frames by the life and power of God."[12] What is David Stark's healing? I'm sure he would say that it is simply divine.

One of the good things that have come from the Toronto Blessing is the arousal of the church. People who try to prove that it is not of the Holy Spirit are now at least admitting that there is a Holy Spirit. Others who refuse to accept divine healing for today are investigating and discovering that while they have found some failures, they are also finding some very positive healings.

Perhaps A.B. Simpson was not too harsh in his assessment.

> Some of the most devoted and distinguished servants of Christ are glad to own Him as their Healer. But I have also noticed that the ecclesiastical straitjacket is the hardest fetter of all, and the fear of man the most inexplorable of all bondage.[13]

There have been those who have criticized most bitterly what has been going on as completely of the flesh at best, and perhaps completely of the devil at worst. That is very easy to do when one sits in an ivory tower, but hasn't personally won a soul to Jesus in many years, or has perhaps never done so. Again the old adage is apropos: The Word without the Spirit tends to dryness; the Spirit without the Word tends to fanaticism.

Sarah Lilliman

Perhaps the most famous account of the Toronto Blessing healings is that of Sarah Lilliman. Her story is given in detail by Guy Chevreau.[14] Research has revealed that Chevreau's account is somewhat flawed,[15] but it does give a general overall picture. Let me give you Chevreau's version with the necessary corrections as stated by authors James Beverley and David Roberts through their detailed research. I will omit those parts of Chevreau's narrative that do not particularly apply to the immediate case.

> In October of 1991, thirteen-year-old Sarah caught what her parents thought was the flu. No sniffles and sneezes, however, could cause her eyesight, very poor from birth, to degenerate further; nor could the flu cause memory loss and cognitive dysfunction.[16]

This leaves the impression that Sarah's problems started in 1991, when actually they began in 1989. Also these problems had been relieved after a month's stay at the world famous Toronto Sick Children's Hospital (SCH) in 1991.[17]

"Testing was done . . . but no medical causes for her symptoms were found."[18]

This is a true statement, but it infers complete mystery. That is not so. The doctors diagnosed many of her problems as psychological in origin. And psychological problems can and often do cause severe physical problems. The key word was "medical," thus giving a false impression.[19]

"As months passed, Sarah lost more and more muscle control, as well as cognitive ability. By October 1993, she was unable to walk, eat, swallow or see."[20]

In actuality, Sarah did show improvement in both eating and swallowing while in the SCH during the following month. Everything did not wait until the "healing" of January 28, 1994.[21]

"In January 1994, she was transferred to Bloorview, a hospital for chronic-care patients, as she needed a mini-hoist to be put to bed."[22]

This took place on December 2, 1993;[23] not an important point, but it does raise doubts about the accuracy of the story. Slips of the tongue are sometimes made in sermons and soon forgotten, but what goes into a book is there for a long time.

On February 27, 1994, Sarah's friend, Rachel, had a vision while "slain in the Spirit" after a message by Randy Clark. Jesus told her to go to Bloorview Hospital the next day and pray for Sarah. "Sarah was in her special wheelchair. . . . She recognized the voices, but could not see or comprehend what was being said to her," says Chevreau.[24] But Beverley states,

> The hospital records make it clear that from December through February, Sarah could see at least partially and had regular conversations (of varying degrees) with her family and hospital staff . . . [regarding] specific and important issues.[25]

As Rachel and her father "interceded over the course of the next two and a half hours, Sarah began to cry, and then shake. Her sight began to come back, and her legs began to move. She slowly began to sit up on her own, and the previous uncontrollable drooling stopped." Almost *two months* later, "on 22 April, 1994, Sarah returned home from Bloorview—no one had any expectation that she would ever leave the chronic-care hospital."[26]

This statement is apparently completely false. There had been a history of decline and improvement ever since 1989. The medical reports of the psychosomatic origins for some of Sarah's physical problems clearly suggested the possibility of recovery.[27]

Four days after returning to her home, Sarah went to a Toronto Airport meeting. She was given this prophecy: "Tonight you will have two healings from God—He will heal your eyes and He will heal your emotions . . . if you will go to the front of the church."[28] This last part of the prophecy was probably "a grasping of straws." Not much had happened to actually show a miracle or even divine healing.

The fact is, in the words of her mother,[29] Sarah "did it because she trusted God." While Jesus often asked people to do something in order for the healing to take place, when they did it, Jesus healed them. This account falls a little short of that. I find it quite easy to accept Rachel's first directions as being from the Lord. I find it very difficult to accept her second "word of knowledge" or prophecy.

Sarah's parents, David and Prim, say that she is still legally blind, and when Sarah went to the meeting on April 26, she did *not* receive two healings from God.[30]

To close this still unsolved issue, I want to quote directly the full article about the "healing of Sarah," as reported in *Spread the Fire*, December 1995, Volume 1, Issue 6, the official voice of the Toronto Airport Christian Fellowship.[31] John Arnott is the editor-in-chief of this magazine:

> An inquiry which speculated whether or not Sarah, the young girl whose healing Guy Chevreau described in *Catch the Fire* truly exists or is a fabrication, was circulated on the Internet. To allay concern, Sarah and her mother were invited to testify on the platform of the "Catch the Fire Again" conference in Toronto on October 5.
>
> Sarah, a girl in her mid-teens, grew up developmentally delayed and near-sighted. At the beginning of 1994 she became ill and lost her sight as well as her ability to walk. She became bedridden and hospitalized. Then friends prayed for her, and she was healed. In her mother's words, "We have our own Sarah back again."
>
> Sarah continues to be developmentally delayed and near-sighted but she recov-

ered from her blindness and an inability
to walk just as Chevreau described.

Whatever the reader may make of the above
seemingly contradictory reports, there are some
things we can assuredly know. First, Sarah is in
need of healing from Jesus by whatever method
God may chose. Second, beliefs built on false
prophecies breed contention and disappoint-
ment. And third, the leadership should not have
tried to vindicate themselves. How refreshing it
would have been if John Arnott had admitted
failure and called the people to pray. It appears to
me that it is more important to be on our knees
in prayer than to be on our hands and knees
roaring like lions.

An incident that supports the contention that
prophecies can be false comes to mind from my
own experience. A friend of mine professed to
having the gift of prophecy. She regularly attended a Wednesday morning meeting in Owen
Sound, Ontario, in which the prophetic voice
was predominant. One morning a distraught lady
came directly from the hospital to the meeting
with a very special prayer request. Her doctor
had informed her that her husband had, at the
worst, only a few hours to live, at the best, only a
few days. Would the ladies pray?

My "prophetess" friend stood up and proclaimed she had a word from the Lord: "This
sickness is not unto death" (John 11:4). The ladies all praised the Lord. If the husband was not

going to die, then why bother to pray? God had spoken. The truth was, there was no need of praying. The husband died just minutes after his wife left the hospital and quite some time before she arrived at the meeting.

This verse portion from John 11:4 is, of course, a very good verse, just like all Bible verses are. Perhaps God did give them that verse for that occasion. If He did, then they had the responsibility to do as Jesus did. He went to the home of Mary and Martha and raised Lazarus from the dead. It is very easy to smugly make a "Bible-verse prophecy," as this lady did. It is quite another thing to accept the responsibility and the consequences. What disturbed me the most was the fact that the "prophetess" was still revered, while God was blamed for letting them down.

> Once I hoped in Jesus,
> Now I know He's mine;
>> Once my lamps were dying,
>> Now they brightly shine;
> Once for death I waited,
> Now His coming hail;
>> And my hopes are anchored,
>> Safe within the vail.[32]

Endnotes

1. *Spread the Fire* (TACF newsletter), ed. John Arnott, January 1995, p. 18.

2. "The Fifth Estate," Canadian Broadcasting Corporation, January 1996 available on video cassette.

3. James A. Beverley, *Holy Laughter and the Toronto Blessing* (Grand Rapids, MI: Zondervan, 1995), p. 105.

4. "Fifth Estate."

5. *Spread the Fire.*

6. Beverley, pp. 106-107.

7. Phone interview with David Stark, March 15, 1996.

8. Ibid.

9. Ibid.

10. A.B. Simpson, *The Gospel of Healing,* (Camp Hill, PA: Christian Publications, 1994), pp. 37-38, 51.

11. The only person in the Bible who accepted gifts from a healing ministry was Gehazi in Second Kings 5, and he, like so many today, suffered because of it.

12. A.B. Simpson, *The Fourfold Gospel* (Camp Hill, PA: Christian Publications, 1984), p. 44.

13. A.B. Simpson, *The Gospel of Healing*, p. 126.

14 Guy Chevreau, *Catch the Fire* (London: Harper-Collins, 1994), pp. 146ff.

15. Beverley, "Faulty Impressions and Mistakes in Fact," pp. 118-119.

16. Chevreau, p. 146.

17. Beverley, p. 118.

18. Chevreau, p. 146.

19. Beverley, p. 118.

20. Chevreau, p. 146.

21. Beverley, p. 118.

22. Chevreau, pp. 146-147.

23. Beverley, p. 118.

24. Chevreau, p. 147.

25. Beverley, p. 118.

26. Chevreau, pp. 147-148.

27. Beverley, p. 118.

28. Chevreau, p. 148.

29. Ibid.

30. Beverley, interview with David and Prim Lilliman, p. 117.

31. *Spread the Fire*, John Arnott, ed., Decemeber 1995, Vol. 1, No. 6, p. 28.

32. A.B. Simpson, "Himself," *Hymns of the Christian Life* (Camp Hill, PA: Christian Publications, 1978), #248.

Chapter 14

Dancing in the Spirit

Wherever I go in North America or across the seas, people have the same questions. The nationality or culture does not seem to alter the situation. It may be Canada's First Nations or America's Hispanic population. It was the same with New Zealand's "reserved" British descendants. In the Philippines the people are quite emotional, while in China no one "wears his heart on his sleeve," but they raised the same queries.

The questions the whole Christian world seems to be asking are "What do you think about being slain in the Spirit?" and "What do you think about dancing in the Spirit?" More recently in India, China and the Philippines, it has been, "What about holy laughter?"

In a previous book, *Handbook on the Holy Spirit*, I discuss "slain in the Spirit," examining the practice in the light of the Scriptures with some practical insights from experience. I want to do the same now with "dancing in the Spirit."

I spoke on this subject at a 1992 men's retreat near Cagayan de Oro in the Philippines. Afterward I was swamped by requests from hundreds of men to put my message in print. Paul Ersando, the chairman of the retreat and a revered attorney from Zamboanga City, stated, "That is the sanest explanation on this subject that I have heard."

"Dancing in the Spirit" is a very prominent part of what we are now calling the Toronto Blessing, so it fits in very well at this point in the history of the church. It appears to me that one of the main objectives of the lengthy musical "worship times" at the Toronto Airport Christian Fellowship is to get as many people as they can into full motion. If this is not the case, then I ask the question, "Why do they inevitably do this right before the offering or the preaching, and then quit?"

To many people, word studies from the Bible are dry and calculating. But it is necessary to have a word study in order to see what God is saying in the Scriptures. While I will be looking at the meaning of words, one does not have to be a Hebrew scholar to get the message of God's Word. Indeed much of the Bible was written in the "street language" of that particular era. One need only take the verses in context to get the real meaning in almost every instance.

"Danced" and "dancing" are used only five times in the New Testament, twice with negatives, twice concerning Herodias' daughter and once (*choros*) referring to the music and chorus singers in the story of the prodigal son. None of these have anything to do with the church.

According to Hebrew scholars, there are a number of words that are translated "dance," "danced," "dances" or "dancing" in the Old Testament. These words occur twenty-two times. I have picked out the most prominent verses, in my opinion, to represent the others. I have transliterated the Hebrew word into English for easy reading.

The reader should keep in mind that the words translated from these various Hebrew words have a number of different meanings: dance, keep festival, turn, twist, a chorus line or choir, jump, leap or skip, move around and finally, a musical instrument.

Chul

First, we turn to Judges 21:19-25 for a very unusual story. Nobody was allowed to give his daughter in marriage to a Benjamite, but they wanted the tribe to continue. A once-a-year plan was made in which the daughters of Shilo would come out to a party and the men of Benjamin would each catch himself a lady to be his wife.[1]

> "If the daughters of Shiloh come out to take part in the dances, then you shall come out of the vineyards and each of you shall catch his wife from the daughters of Shiloh. . . ." And the sons of

Benjamin did so, and took wives according to their number from those who danced, whom they carried away. (Judges 21:21, 23)

The word in both verses is *chul*, which can be translated "dance," "turn" or "twist."[2] The meaning is obvious. The Benjamites were enticed by the dancing of the girls and picked out the ones they wanted. It is very interesting to notice the last verse in the chapter: "In those days there was no king in Israel; everyone did what was right in his own eyes" (Judges 21:25).

The Bible does not tell us to take part in these types of parties. It merely says that the daughters of Shilo did it. It leaves us to judge the consequences. These young virgin ladies received ungodly husbands for their actions.

Chagag

Chagag in First Samuel 30:16 literally means "to keep festival or to keep the pilgrim feast."[3] While there may have been dancing at the feast, that has to be read into the story. The meaning of the word does not indicate such, nor does the context. It was the celebration of victory when David defeated the Amalekites and the soldiers brought home so much spoil (1 Samuel 30:1-17). It was not a worship service. It was a party. And if they danced, they danced. It is not a verse that can be used pro or con.

Mecholah

Another Hebrew word can be translated as "dance," "dancing," or "a chorus line or choir." It is *mecholah*.[4] The context is needed to give us the proper meaning. In Exodus 15:20 we read, "And Miriam the prophetess, Aaron's sister, took the timbrel in her hand, and all the women went out after her with timbrels and with dancing." Notes in the margin of the New American Standard Bible read, "Literally, dances."

The next verse tells us what they "danced": "And Miriam answered them: 'Sing to the LORD, for He is highly exalted; The horse and his rider He has hurled into the sea'" (Exodus 15:21). So this word, which can also be translated "a chorus line or choir," should be read as such.

The reader might say, "That's a mighty short song for such a big event as coming through the Red Sea on dry ground." However, Miriam is simply starting them into the new song that Moses had just given them as recorded in Exodus 15:1-17. Note that "Miriam's verse" is exactly the same as the first verse that Moses wrote. She is not starting *her* new song. She is starting the Song of Moses. It is a song of worship to their (and our) great God for who He is. It is a song of praise for what He has done.[5] They may have danced, but the context is not sufficiently clear to claim this is so.

Machol

In Psalm 150, that finale of praises, there is another word, *machol*. It is similar to the word just previously explained, but not the same. While *machol* can mean all the things that *macholah* does, it means a little more. It can also mean "a musical instrument."[6]

In Psalm 150:3-5, we are told to praise God with 1) trumpet; 2) harp; 3) lyre; 4) timbrel; 5) dancing; 6) stringed instruments; 7) pipe; 8) loud cymbals; and 9) resounding cymbals. You will notice that in the exact middle, there is "dancing" or *machol*. What is the context? Everything around that word is a musical instrument. Our calling to be "a workman . . . handling accurately the word of truth" (2 Timothy 2:15) demands that we call this "dancing" a musical instrument.

This is the psalm that most exponents of "dancing in the Spirit" will turn to, to prove their point, so I have looked at it a little further. In the translation that John Calvin uses in his commentary, he names the nine instruments as follows: trumpet, psaltery, harp, timbrel, *pipe*, chords, organ, cymbals of sound and cymbals of jubilation (italics mine).[7] Calvin says,

> The Hebrew word employed, is often . . . rendered "dance"; but this is not its meaning. It denotes . . . some fistular wind instrument of music, with holes, as a flute, pipe, or fife.[8]

202

"I know of no place in the Bible," says Adam Clark, "where *machol* . . . means dance of any kind; it constantly means some kind of pipe."[9]

Actually *machol* can denote another kind of ancient musical instrument, as well as the one just noted. William Smith calls it

> a musical instrument of percussion, supposed to have been used by the Hebrews at an early period of history. In the great Hallelujah Psalm (Psalm 150) the sacred poet exhorts mankind to praise Jehovah in His sanctuary with all kinds of music; and among the instruments mentioned at 3rd, 4th and 5th verses is found *machol*. It is generally believed to have been made of metal, open like a ring: it had many small bells attached to its border, and was played at weddings and merry-makings by women, who accompanied it with voice.[10]

After weighing the evidence, one has to conclude that Psalm 150 does not give a basis for men to shuffle their feet nor women to swivel their hips in church. They can do that if they want to, but they cannot base it on the Psalms.

Raqad

There is also *raqad*. Here there is no mistaking

the meaning. It can only be translated "dance" or "skip."[11] It is recorded in Ecclesiastes 3:4: "A time to weep and a time to laugh; a time to mourn and a time to dance." If we take this to be an order from God, rather than the signs of the emptiness of the life of natural man, then we must also obey all the twenty-eight orders in the list, which includes "a time to kill . . . a time to throw stones . . . and a time to hate."

Karkar

Finally, we come to King David. How often the writer has heard, "If it was OK for David, it must be OK for us." Let us look at the story as recorded in Second Samuel 6. The ark of the covenant has just arrived at David's city bringing much joy and excitement to all concerned.

> And David was dancing before the LORD with all his might, and David was wearing a linen ephod. . . . Then it happened as the ark of the LORD came into the city of David that Michal the daughter of Saul looked out of the window and saw King David leaping and dancing before the LORD; and she despised him in her heart. . . . When David returned to bless his household, Michal the daughter of Saul came out to meet David and said, "How the king of Israel has distinguished himself to-

day! He uncovered himself today in the eyes of his servants' maids as one of the foolish ones shamelessly uncovers himself!" (2 Samuel 6:14, 16, 20)

The word in both cases here is *karkar* which can be translated as "dance," "move around," "skip" and "leap" or "jump."[12] It is quite obvious what David was doing. He was so thrilled that he "let himself go," just like the man at the Beautiful Gate in Acts 3:8.

I direct the reader next to First Chronicles 15:29: "And it happened when the ark of the covenant of the LORD came to the city of David, that Michal the daughter of Saul looked out of the window, and saw King David leaping and making merry; and she despised him in her heart." The word here is *raqad*, which can be translated as "dancing," "skipping" or "leaping" as the NASB puts it. Second Samuel and First Chronicles use different Hebrew words, but the meanings are identical. So we see that David was not playing an instrument. He was not singing—at least the Scripture gives no indication that he was. David was indeed dancing and jumping in his worship and praise. Now we have the whole story.

David was out on the streets of Jerusalem rejoicing in the Lord. He went dancing and jumping. And he lost control of himself in all the excitement. (Does this sound familiar?) In his jumping and leaping about, his ephod came loose and he was exposed in front of the ladies. He was out of control. Again I come back to the fruit of the Spirit, part of which is self-control, as we have previously noted (Galatians 5:22-23).

This is not a man who is Spirit-filled at this point: he lacked the fruit of the Spirit. Furthermore, when he went home to his wife, they had a spat. Love was not shown; no joy, no peace and no kindness. (Remember that this is the wife that David demanded of Saul in First Samuel 18. Saul wanted David to have Merab as his wife, but David opted for Michal.) But after the spat over David's notorious dance, it appears that they never had relations again (2 Samuel 6:23).

There are some that would argue that Michal was stricken with barrenness because God was pleased with David's dancing as a form of worship. I cannot hold this view. This view advocates that God was pleased with David "uncovering himself today in the eyes of his servants' maids as one of the foolish ones shamelessly uncovers himself." The NIV reads, "disrobing in the sight of the slave girls of his servants as any vulgar fellow would" (2 Samuel 6:20).

In Moffatt's translation we find, "exposing himself before women, before his own menials, as any loose fellow would expose himself indecently." The KJV has it thus: "who uncovered himself to day in the eyes of the handmaids of his servants, as one of the vain fellows shamelessly uncovereth himself!" The Good News Bible states it in street language, "He exposed himself like a fool in the sight of the servant girls of his officials" (2 Samuel 6:20).

Since there is some controversy concerning this event, I want to add just one more translation. The New King James Version states, "uncovering himself today in the eyes of the maids of his servants as one of the base fellows shamelessly [margin, openly] uncovers himself."

At this point one might argue that God was pleased with the dancing but not the exposure. That could be a valid point, but I think we cannot separate the two when we use David as an example of dancing in the church commonly called "dancing in the Spirit." It may have begun as a spiritual dance, but it later became uncontrolled, violating the ninth fruit of the Spirit—self-control.

Now if we want to take David as an example, we will get out on the street in our home city, leap and jump and praise the Lord, rip off our clothes while doing so, and then go home to our mates, but never live together again. This is roughly what happened in the instance of David's so-called "dancing in the Spirit."

I was asked to speak on this subject in my home area. Some people were not delighted with my message. I had stated that I had investigated a number of churches that practiced "dancing in the Spirit." I found that if the church had been doing this for extended periods of times, there was always sexual immorality and often with clergy as well as laity.

I was accosted following the service by lay persons and a pastor. I was informed that the fastest growing church in our city had dancing in every service. I simply replied that the church was quite young and we should keep watch on it to see what would happen in the future.

Little did I know how prophetic my observations were. Within two weeks the news was all over town. The married senior pastor of that "fastest growing church" had been having affairs for sixteen years. "Be sure your sin will find you out" (Numbers 32:23) is just as valid for us today as when it was written. The pastor had a son pastoring in another city, where they had "dancing in the Spirit" as well. The following week he was found to be in sexual sin.

And the pastor who accosted me? Within a year, I read the story in the newspaper of his molesting young girls. Part of the punishment meted out was that he could no longer work in an area that involved contact with young girls. He had already lost his associate pastorate status and at the time of this writing has continued in secular employment and has not endeavored to reenter public ministry.

Often the question comes, "If David could do it, then why can't we?" Well, there were a number of things that David did that are a far cry from being Christlike. To get Michal to be his wife, David killed 200 Philistines so he could give Saul a dowry of 200 foreskins as recorded in

First Samuel 18:25-27. Already he showed over-zealousness. Saul had asked for only 100.

Are we to follow David's example in committing adultery with our neighbor's spouse? In this case it was Bathsheba in Second Samuel 11. Are we to try to cover up our sin by having the innocent spouse killed? Are we to try to vindicate ourselves when confronted with our sin, rather than repenting, as David did in Second Samuel 12?

Are we to follow David's example by having multiple mates? Five of his wives are named: Michal, Ahinoam, Abigail, Maacah and Bathsheba. And besides all these, we read, "David took more concubines and wives from Jerusalem, after he came from Hebron; and more sons and daughters were born to David" (2 Samuel 5:13).

I once was a member of a board where a staff member was asked to give us a devotional. He chose Psalm 26:1: "Vindicate me, O Lord, for I have walked in my integrity; And I have trusted in the Lord without wavering." In his message, the speaker told us that if David was able to talk about his integrity, perhaps we judge people too harshly who have fallen, particularly in sexual sin.

The speaker, however, overlooked a very important point. David was telling of his integrity before his fall into sin.[13] By the time we get to Psalm 51, David is writing about his repentance following his fall into various types of sin. It was after his repentance recorded here that David becomes a great man of God.

It is quite noticeable that David never talked about his integrity again after his fall. Asaph wrote of it in Psalm 78:72, but David did not. If you must take David as your example, you should not do it before he cries out to God, "Create in me a clean heart, O God, and renew a steadfast spirit within me" (Psalm 51:10).

There likely will always be churches that promote "dancing in the Spirit." It looks like it is with us to stay. At this time the Toronto Blessing features it at nearly every service. They often call it "pogoing," as well as dancing. What I would like all these churches to do is this: Stop calling it by that non-scriptural term. Just call it "dancing," because there is no such thing as "dancing in the Spirit," only *dancing*, period.

And they should be prepared to cope with immorality at any moment. The practice as I have pointed out through the Scriptures and through observation is certainly not a sign of spirituality, but one of carnality. Rather than dancing, we should tell the Lord:

> I'm weary of sinning and stumbling,
>> Repenting and falling again;
> I'm tired of resolving and striving,
>> And finding the struggle so vain.
> I long for an arm to uphold me,
>> A will that is stronger than mine;

A Saviour to cleanse me and fill me,
And keep me by power divine.[14]

Endnotes

1. Paul P. Enns, *Bible Study Commentary* (Grand Rapids, MI: Zondervan, 1982), p. 144.

2. Robert Young, *Young's Analytical Concordance* (Nashville, TN: Thomas Nelson, 1982), p. 220.

3. Ibid., p. 220.

4. Ibid., p. 220.

5. C.H. McIntosh, *Notes on Exodus*, (New York: Loizeaux Brothers, Inc., n.d.), p. 191.

6. James Compter Gray and George M. Adams, eds. *Gray and Adams Bible Commentary* (Grand Rapids, MI: Zondervan, n.d.), p. 733.

7. John Calvin, *Calvin's Commentary* (Grand Rapids, MI: Baker, reprinted 1984), p. 455.

8. Ibid., p. 318.

9. Ibid., p. 310, note 2.

10. William Smith, *A Dictionary of the Bible* (Chicago: Fleming H. Revell, n.d.), p. 131.

11. Young, p. 220.

12. Ibid.

13. David Dickson, *A Commentary on the Psalms* (Minneapolis, MN: Klock and Klock Christian Publications, 1980), p. 136. Dickson states, "David . . . being exiled from the house of God," certainly not a king, as he was in Psalm 51, showing repentence. J.M. Neale and R.F. Littledale, *A Commentary on the Psalms* (New York: AMS Press Company, 1976), p. 361. Neale and Littledale say, "The Psalm is one of

David's earliest writing . . . classed with Psalm eight." Spurgeon puts Psalm 26 at "the time of the assassination of Ishbosheth," the son of Saul, as recorded in Second Samuel 4:2-9. David's sin with Bathsheba is recorded in Second Samuel 11, and his repentence in Second Samuel 12. Matthew Henry states, "It is probable that David penned this Psalm when he was persecuted by Saul." While the commentators do not agree to the time of the writing, all seem to agree that it was before David became king, and therefore before his fall into sin.

14. A.B. Simpson, "I Want to Be Holy," *Hymns of the Christian Life* (Camp Hill, PA: Christian Publications, 1978), #235.

Chapter 15

Holy Laughter

There are two things in particular that have been constants in the life of the Church. The first is good expository preaching; the second is fads. The former has continued throughout the centuries. Fads come and go. It seems both are needed.

Expository preaching keeps the church strong. The fads keep the church excited. There is no substitute for the preaching; the fads are substitutes in themselves. They are not essentially bad, but they are very poor substitutes for the working of the Holy Spirit.

When I became a pastor in the early 1950s, Sunday school was the fad. Most evangelical churches ran Sunday school contests. My church won an international contest in 1953. The Sunday school had to be bigger than your morning worship service or you were a dud.

There was also the day of the evangelistic crusade. Then came prophetic conferences. Some people began to dress in white robes and climb mountains to wait for Christ's return. The atomic bomb had scared people into becoming Christians. Now the populace was accustomed to the danger, and nothing could scare them—not even going to hell.

Along came the "Jesus People," the demonstrations and the Sunday school bus. If the church parking lot didn't look orange, you had better do something about it. Revival meetings became a way of life in the 1970s, which gave a great increase in Bible college attendance for a few years, as was discussed in chapter 7.

But crusade evangelism was soon "out," unless of course Billy Graham was coming to town. Then the opponents of crusades became promoters for the meetings and afterward went back to the old fads again. Friendship evangelism became the fad of the day and is still with us, filling our churches with people who readily said "yes"—often without tears, sometimes without repentance.

Dr. Arnold Cook, in the keynote address to the Canadian Revival Fellowship's twenty-fifth anniversary, said, "We have smart preaching . . . but toothless altar calls," calling it "anemic evangelism." He further described it as

> . . . a soft-sell approach that avoids the whole issue of Lordship and is therefore basically a program of self-improvement as opposed to life-changing in the true sense.[1]

Tongues again came to the fore, rippled through the church for a while and then slackened once more as dancing became the rage for a few years. But that has been overpowered by laughter, which the church is now calling "holy laughter."

I have been a fun Christian for many years. I enjoy myself in the ministry. I do not minister because I find it rewarding, although it is that. My heart aches for lost souls. It drives me to preach and testify. I have used many ways to attract people to Christ, both as a pastor from 1952 to 1972 and as an evangelist from 1972 to the present. I have never used laughter as one of these ways. But laughter is the most recent fad, and it is doing a good job of getting people's attention. It will doubtless fade again into near oblivion, and something else will take its place.

Most fads are quite harmless. I'm not so sure about that which is being heralded as "holy laughter." I am delighted to see church people happy. Church ought to do special things for each of us. There is healing power in laughter, as I explained in chapter 8. But to have uncontrollable laughter may be dangerous. I have for many years been opposed to "let yourself go and take what comes."

The devil would find it very difficult to counterfeit some fads. Take, for instance, the Sunday school bus. How can the devil counterfeit the bus itself? Either you have one or you don't (although I have seen some that hardly qualify as a bus). But the devil does have counterfeit laughter, and when he sees it, he too sits back and laughs.

There are some areas that need special care. In *Dance Your Way to God*, we read, "Just be joyful. God is not serious. This world cannot fit with a theological God. So let this be your constant reminder. You have to dance your way to God. You have to laugh your way to God."[2] This does not come out of the Toronto Blessing. It comes from the Oregon guru, Bhagwhan Shree Rajneesh.

He was often referred to as being drunk on the divine. He encouraged people to come and drink from him. His "spiritual wine" was often passed along to others by a single touch of his hand to a parishioner's head. Many of these would fall to the floor in total ecstasy after the encounter.[3]

I do not say that this type of thing is happening in what has been referred to as the "laughing revival." What I am saying is that there needs to be control so that this type of devilish counterfeit will not happen, if it has not already taken place.

From *The Gospel of Healing* we may gain some extra insights:

> *The same results as are claimed for faith in healing of disease are also said to follow the practices of spiritism, animism, clairvoyance and the like.* . . . These manifestations are often real and superhuman. They are "the spirits of devils, working miracles"

(Revelation 16:14). They are the revived forces of the Egyptian magicians, the Grecian oracles, the Roman haruspices, the Indian fakirs. They are not divine. They are less than omnipotent, but they are more than human.

Our Lord expressly warned us of them and told us to test them, not by their power but by their fruits—their holiness, humility and homage to the name of Jesus and the Word of God.[4]

Laughter is mentioned forty times in the Bible. This should be sufficient to work up a good sermon on the subject. However, almost all the verses have to do with sadness and sorrow. There is much more about joy, but laughter and joy are two completely different subjects.

The dictionary describes joy as "a strong feeling of pleasure, gladness, delight, rapture and bliss, especially the bliss of heaven."[5] "Laugh" means

> to make the sounds and motions of the face and body that show mirth, amusement, scorn, revelry, etc., sometimes employed by birds, such as the mocking bird, and animals, such as the laughing hyena.[6]

The very meaning of these words may speak volumes concerning the subject at hand. Even on a scriptural basis we cannot equate the two. It is not fair to the Word of God to say that holy laughter and joy are synonymous. But rather than do another word study, I want to lay out what we should expect when revival comes. For this I borrow from a publication from Life Action Ministries, March 1995:

1. *God's Word will be exalted and authoritative over man's experience.* To elevate (or even equate) man's experience with the authority of God's Word is to become vulnerable to confusion and grave spiritual error. This is not to say that revival will bypass human experience and emotion, but that our experience must always be subordinate and subject to the absolute truth of God's Word.

2. *There will be intense conviction of sin, leading to repentance.* Confronted by the holiness of God, conviction of sin intensifies and breeds in us an urgency for repentance. It is [pictured in] Isaiah's [words:] "Woe is me, for I am ruined! Because I am a man of unclean lips, and I live among people of unclean lips; for my eyes have seen the King, the LORD of hosts" (Isaiah 6:5).

Paul put it this way, "For the sorrow that is according to the will of God produces a repentance without regret, leading to salvation; but the sorrow of the world produces death" (2 Corinthians 7:10). Revival brings an intensity of God's grace which both demands and enables the forsaking of sin. We depart the well-worn pathway of personal failure and embark on the "Highway of Holiness."

3. *Humility and brokenness will be evident.* In seasons of genuine revival, the passion for purity, a clear conscience, and, above all, God's glory becomes so intense that no price is too great to pay. Although not necessarily enjoyable, embracing humility and experiencing brokenness are the only ways to encounter God's holiness. Just as Jesus, "who for the joy set before Him endured the cross" (Hebrews 12:2), so we must endure brokenness before God's joy can be restored in us.

4. *There will be deliberate acts of reconciliation and restitution.* No longer content to "let bygones be bygones," there will be a God-given zeal to obtain and maintain a clear conscience. Jesus said, "If therefore you . . . remember that your brother has something against you, . . . first be reconciled to your brother, and then come and present your offering" (Matthew 5:23-24).

Paul said, "In view of this, I also do

my best to maintain always a blameless conscience both before God and before men" (Acts 24:16). No longer will we bring our gifts of worship and service to the altar, while harboring hurt, anger or bitterness.

5. *There will be a growing interest in prayer.* Just as prayer precedes revival, so also prayer maintains revival. When God is present, He cannot be ignored. Hunger for intimacy with Him is heightened and finds expression through prayer. Being in His presence will become the delight of our life.

6. *Joy will be untainted and pure.* In seasons of revival, the desire to be entertained and to feel good is revealed for what it really is—a cheap imitation of godly joy. Biblical prayers for revival speak of joy as a thing to be desired and as the by-product of a genuine move of God. "Wilt Thou not Thyself revive us again, that Thy people may rejoice in Thee?" (Psalm 85:6). Joy, rather than entertainment, will become a hallmark of our worship. God Himself will take the "center-stage," and the Lord Jesus will reign as the sole object of our adoration.

7. *Evangelism will flourish.* History bears witness that more souls are ushered into the kingdom during seasons

of revival than at any other time. As God's Spirit rests upon His church with renewed power, her witness to the world becomes credible. Once bound in fear of rejection, self-love and indifference, God's people find new freedom, desire and faith to share the gospel.[7]

If the "holy laughter" of the Toronto Blessing promotes these seven vital points, then let us have more laughter. I do not think it does. But I do know that the "long faces" in many evangelical churches do not promote these points either. I have heard all too often, the long drawn out put-down: "Brother, we may not have quantity, but we have quality." It is my opinion that quality attracts quantity.

> Burn on O fire of God, burn on
>   Till all my dross is burned away,
>   Till earth and sin and self are gone,
>   And I can stand the testing day.[8]

Endnotes

1. Doug Koop quoting Dr. Arnold Cook in "Broken Cisterns Leak Revival Power," *Christian Week*, March 26, 1996, p. 2.
2. Danny Aguirre, Spiritual Counterfeit Project Newsletter, Fall 1994, 19:2, p. 14.
3. Ibid.

4. A.B. Simpson, *The Gospel of Healing* (Camp Hill, PA: Christian Publications, 1986), pp. 43-44.

5. *The World Book Dictionary*, Vol. 1 (Chicago: Field Enterprises Educational Corporation, 1973), p. 1128.

6. Ibid., Vol. 2, pp. 1174-1175.

7. "Revival Report" (an open public letter circulated en masse), Life Action Ministries, March 1995, Byron Paulus, ex. dir.

8. A.B. Simpson, "Burn On!" *Hymns of the Christian Life* (Camp Hill, PA: Christian Publications, 1978), #246.

Chapter 16

In the Vernacular

It is incumbent upon a speaker to speak in a manner that the audience understands. As a pastor for many years in five Canadian provinces, I found I had to "change gears" wherever I went.

Furthermore, I accepted small struggling churches, saw them revived, started new churches as a result of the revival and then moved to the next city. In doing this, I should have taken on extra staff to keep from burning out, but I was always a solo pastor. That meant I had to speak to the youth in their language and speak at the old-fashioned prayer meeting in the language of the seniors.

Then there were always new converts who thought that a "prayer warrior"[1] was a converted Indian. Or that to "have oil" on you[2] meant you were a smooth operator, instead of being God's anointed servant. In central Canada, people said I ran like a deer. In western Canada, I ran like an antelope. In eastern Canada, I ran "right fast." One must keep up with the language at hand.

In ministering with Canada's First Nations peoples and overseas, much of the time I have an interpreter and must use language that does not baffle him. A Kiwi knows all about sheep, but an Inuit has never seen one. Many readers will not know that a Kiwi is a New Zealander, and an Inuit is wrongly called an "Eskimo" in almost every encyclopedia. The term "Eskimo" is a racial slur.[3]

The Toronto Blessing and the events leading up to it have coined some new words and phrases. Some of them will remain; some are passing fads; some I hope will disappear quickly. There are some that are offensive. A number of others depict a corruption of certain Bible verses, such as "let the bubble activate your belly." This supposedly comes from

> If any man is thirsty, let him come to Me and drink. He who believes in Me, as the Scripture said, "From his innermost being [out of his belly, KJV] shall flow rivers of living water." (John 7:37-38)

Almost all phraseology used by the Toronto Blessing concerning the Holy Spirit describes Him as a thing. They almost completely depersonalize the Holy Spirit by the use of the pronoun "it." This is a grievance to the Holy Spirit, and we are warned not to grieve Him (Hebrews 3:7-11). This warning and the personality of the

Holy Spirit are discussed much more fully in
Handbook on the Holy Spirit.[4]

However, many of the new words and phrases
are merely the language of our day or phrases
coined and used by various charismatic movements. Here is a partial listing as I have taken
them from public services, video cassettes, books,
articles and newsletters. There is no order of importance.

Get 'em, Jesus.
Hit him, Lord.
Let the bubble activate your belly.
Don't pray. Laugh.
Higher in the Spirit realm.
We don't worship the Bible, just the
    God of the Bible.
We can't anchor the experiences to the
    Bible.
There are manifestations that there is
    not Scripture for.
Looking for more zip.
Everything broke out there.
Stuck to the floor for hours.
When the Lord showed up.
Isn't God bigger than His book?
Starting to be empowered prophetically.
Doing carpet time.
Things have already broken out.
Getting drunk in the Spirit.
Some people's Trinity is Father, Son
    and Holy Book.

It is easy to transfer it to other churches.
Flung the Holy Spirit across the room.
The Spirit broke out powerfully.
Things broke out there.
Prophesied powerfully.
God has told us.
Give the anointing away.
Touched by this thing.
The Word becomes the Living Word
      when it speaks to us.
Some people don't believe in the Holy
      Spirit, because they don't know
      what it is, and you can't see it.
Don't try to reason it. Just take it.
I got zapped.
Let it bubble your belly.
Laughing revival.
Their drunken condition became their
      testimony.
Holy Ghost bartender.
Fax the laughter to your church.
Hit with revival.
Soak her, Lord.
God touched down here.
Revival broke out.
Holy laughter is the joy of the Lord.
Don't analyze. Just receive.
Praise the Lord and pass the new wine.
Either You come down here and touch
      me, or I will come up there and
      touch You.

Holy laughter is the last days expression of the Holy Spirit.
Soaked in the Spirit.
Plug into heaven's electrical supply.
Plug other people into your supply.
It is immediately transferable to other people.
Getting hit with the Spirit.
Thrashed on the floor: massaged by Jesus.
Lay hands on everything that moves.
Cackling convulsions.
Glued to the floor.
They were struck dumb.
Check your mind at the door.
Holy laughter is awesome.
Get into this thing.
The roaring is prophetic.
The crowing is prophetic.
We can't stop this thing.
Falls to the ground and roars like a lion.
Giggle with the Holy One.
Powerful miracles.
Under the power.
Do you want it? Then take it.
I'm a blower. When the Spirit of God hits, I blow and blow and blow.
The Wind just jets right out of me.
I'm a rooster crower.
Go ahead; let the bubble out your belly.
Hoo! Hoo! Hoo!
That's called Holy Ghost aerobics.

Joy! Joy! Joy! Don't pray! Laugh!
It's not a prayer meeting! Joy! Joy! Joy!
Don't try to validate with Scripture.
It's a new thing.
Get a drink of this.
Holy laughter.
Powerful healings.
It's greater than Pentecost.

Some of these sayings will strike the readers in different ways. What may be offensive in one part of the world might be well received in another. Let the reader sort them out. But in the light of Scripture, the last one that I have cited is the most repulsive to me. How can what we have been seeing be greater than Pentecost? Pentecost required unity. We have seen a split as I show in the next chapter. And let us look at the fruit.

Peter's first sermon brought in a harvest of "about three thousand" (Acts 2:41). The next recorded meeting brought another great response: "the number of the *men* came to be about five thousand" (Acts 4:4, italics mine). Then in Acts 5:14 we read, "And all the more believers in the Lord, *multitudes of men and women,* were constantly added to their number" (italics mine). Also there were continuing results: ". . . *a great many of the priests* were becoming obedient to the faith" (Acts 6:7, italics mine). Then whole communities believed: *"And all who lived at Lydda and Sharon* saw him, and they turned to the Lord" (Acts 9:35, italics mine).

The Toronto Blessing has seen nothing like that. And neither have I. The only person that God has used from the time of "the twelve" (Acts 6:2, 1 Corinthians 15:5) until now, with visible results like that, is still with us today. He is Billy Graham, the man who has never allowed the spectacular to overshadow the Word of God. He was the preacher in Toronto when John Arnott took Jesus to be his Savior.

Ironically, Billy Graham was back in Toronto, in the Skydome this time, for another crusade in 1995. This was at the height of the phenomena at Toronto Airport Christian Fellowship. In all the books I have read and the "colossal mound" of other materials concerning the Toronto Blessing, I find no mention of the Billy Graham crusade. And that is where there was unity among the churches and a mighty harvest of souls.

> Oh, how sweet the glorious message
> Simple faith may claim;
> Yesterday, today, forever,
> Jesus is the same.
> Still He loves to save the sinful,
> Heal the sick and lame,
> Cheer the mourner, still the tempest—
> Glory to His name![6]

Endnotes

1. This term is derived from Ephesians 6:10-20.

2. This term is derived from Psalm 133:2.

3. Elmer Harp, Jr., "Eskimo," *The World Book Encyclopedia,* Vol. 6, p. 278.

4. Robert J. Kuglin, *Handbook on the Holy Spirit* (Camp Hill, PA: Christian Publications, Inc., 1996), pp. 68ff.

5. A.B. Simpson, "Yesterday, Today, Forever," *Hymns of the Christian Life* (Camp Hill, PA: Christian Publications, 1978), #119.

Chapter 17

The New Child Is Born

Earlier in this book I told about one of John Wimber's new encounters with God. It was based on Sarah's question: "Shall I indeed bear a child, when I am so old?" (Genesis 18:13).[1] He seemed to lump this together with the festival word *Pentecost*.[2] This is a long way from being hermeneutically sound.

According to Wimber, this was interpreted to mean that a new day was dawning and that the Vineyard movement would give birth to a new thing, a new Pentecost. This perhaps helped to give birth to some of the "prophecies" cited in chapters 3 and 4 and the endeavor to bring them to pass by the Toronto Airport Christian Fellowship.

John Wimber had visited the fellowship early in the unusual manifestation period of the Airport church. He had requested that some control be put on the activities. But he also showed some perplexity about what was happening. He had said, "There is no scriptural support for such phenomena and no historic precedent. So I feel no obligation to try to explain it. It's just phenomena. It's just people responding to God."[3]

Previously Dr. Wimber had said that "such behaviors (making animal noises, in particular) were considered demonic in the past at the Anaheim Vineyard." Later he claimed that those same manifestations could have been from God.[4]

There seems to be some confusion over what went on during the earlier negotiations concerning the animal manifestations. Quoting different people only leads to more confusion. However, we do know this. On December 4, 1995, Wimber notified Creation House, Lake Mary, Florida, that "he wanted his endorsement removed from future editions of the book,"[5] meaning *The Father's Blessing* by John Arnott.

Wimber says, "I was not happy with the book, but at first I thought it was appropriate to endorse it since John Arnott was attempting to deal with corrections." But within three weeks of the book's release, Arnott made several public statements and published two articles attributing prophetic significance to animal behavior. Wimber concludes, "This was more than we could handle."[6]

From *Charisma*'s People and Events, February 1996, came this report:

> Toronto Airport Vineyard Fellowship, birthplace of a renewal that has spread throughout the world over the

past two years, has been ousted from the Association of Vineyard Churches (AVC) over what the denomination calls "exotic practices" in renewal services.

The division occurred despite the pleading of Airport Vineyard supporters who asked Wimber for time to work out a resolution.

"Wimber said they weren't there for discussion; they were there to make an announcement," said Bud Williams, pastor of Evangel Temple, an independent charismatic church in Toronto. [Williams attended the meeting in support of John Arnott.] "The charges didn't warrant this kind of rash decision," he said.

To the members of the board (AVC), however, the decision to release the Toronto church was not a rash one. In September 1994, the denomination's position on the renewal was hashed out in an emergency session of the board and distributed to all Vineyard pastors. "Over a 14-month period," Wimber said, "the Toronto leaders repeatedly violated the guidelines contained in the position report."

The twenty-member board voted unanimously to release Toronto from the denomination.

The issues center in part on the unusual animal-like behavior—such as roaring or barking. . . . Wimber said Arnott and his staff were repeatedly warned not to promote, encourage or theologize the animal behavior and the accompanying sounds.

Arnott believes the dispute over the animal sounds was fueled by media reports emphasizing the strange behavior, which he says rarely occurs . . . "and in almost every case, it's been of God."[7]

In the *National and International Religion Report* came word that

Wimber and Vineyard administrators Todd Hunter, Bob Fulton, and Gary Best traveled from AVC headquarters in Anaheim, California to Toronto to announce their action Dec. 5. The renewal has been "a blessing to many and a wonderful work of God," the association said. "[But the AVC cannot support] any exotic practices that are extra biblical."[8]

The *Toronto Star*, December 10, 1995 reported:

The major disagreement, the denomination said, was over Arnott's emphasis on Christians being dramatically filled by the Holy Spirit before they were adequately equipped to evangelize, start new congregations, and minister to the poor and others. Manifestations of being filled by the Holy Spirit, Arnott said, included uncontrollable laughing, shaking, loud moaning, and falling to the floor. There have also been reports of healings.[9]

"You need to give yourself permission to take time to soak in the presence of the Lord," Arnott told worshipers in Pasadena, California on Friday, December 8, 1995. While he spoke, a woman writhed on the floor in front of him, laughing uncontrollably. "I'm here to say that if you will soak in the presence of the Holy Spirit a couple of hours a day...."[10]

This Pasadena church, where Che Ahn is the senior pastor, was the first to join Arnott in the support of the Toronto church, doing so the day before the December 8 meeting.[11]

While some writers maintained that the separation was amicable, there does seem to be some tension. At first, the Toronto leadership reported that "unity" was the key and that churches were uniting as never before. Arnott, in the preface to *Catch the Fire* states:

It is so life-giving that denominational differences have melted into obscurity, as a fresh love for Jesus has become preeminent; leaders of every denominational persuasion have come and drunk deeply of this fresh outpouring. The Holy Spirit is the only true unifier![12]

Now we read different words from the lips of this same man. In the January 2, 1996 issue of *Christian Week*, Arnott states, "One thing that pains me is that one of the highest Vineyard virtues is to model mercy and grace. But in our own family, we can't seem to make it work."[13]

"I feel like I got thrown out of Vineyard for a book that John Wimber endorsed," says Arnott in *Charisma*, February 1996.[14] The issue was the animal noises. He denied that anyone on his staff encouraged the practice and further that AVC never communicated any clear warning that the church was in danger of being dismissed.

Very early in the "renewal" Arnott had stated that the church worked within the Episcopal church governing system.[15] It seems that he only worked within the system until he disagreed with his overseers. And that is not working within a system, that is "using the system" as long as you agree with your leaders. It falls far short of the command, "Obey your leaders, and submit to them" (Hebrews 13:17).

Wimber says, "We love them and desire only the best for them as they pursue what they believe to be God's will for their lives."[16]

Arnott accepted the Association of Vineyard Church's decision and asked to be released with the association's "blessing."[17] This sounds like a cordial parting of the ways, from their official communiqués. However, language at other times seems to give more than a small hint of bitterness. Vineyard's midwest regional overseer, Happy Lehman, posted a letter on the Internet stating that they were attempting "to bring some degree of order to the pastoring and packaging of the Toronto Blessing." They also believed that certain misunderstandings of the end times expressed by the Airport Vineyard leaders are neither biblical nor helpful.[18]

Part of the above indicates that the Airport Vineyard was caught by complete surprise in the decision to "fly solo" as *Christian Week* so aptly put it.[19] However, we find that "for now, Arnott is continuing with plans to assemble an advisory board to oversee the renewal, *plans that were in place several months before the December meeting*" (italics mine).[20]

If the December 5, 1995[21] ouster by the AVC came as such a surprise, why was Arnott making the preparations for a new organization before that time? Or did Wimber discover what was happening and decide to take the scriptural steps referred to later?

It appears to me that most scriptural discipline can only take place while the party is still part of the official organization. To wait would be too late.

A long time ago one of my overseers told me to "always remember that time is a wonderful healer." I did not believe him then, and I do not believe him now. It is true that the wound will heal over. But if it heals with the poison still inside, that poison will affect the body until it is removed. The only lasting solution is to confess, forsake and forgive. I did not say "forget." It is impossible for the human brain to deliberately forget.

Arnott says, "We're confused by the dismissal, but we've been confused before, and we've been hurt before."[22] That does not really sound all that amicable, especially combining his words with the following: "We were removed without due process." He also accused the Vineyard leadership of "not getting an accurate picture of what was taking place at the renewal meetings."[23]

Wimber saw it in a different light. "We see this as a Matthew-18 issue, that we have been sinned against."[24] These are strong words coming from the leader of a fast-growing denomination to a pastor who just two years previously was virtually unknown. Here is the Scripture that Wimber used:

And if your brother sins, go and reprove him in private; if he listens to you, you have won your brother. But if he will not listen to you, take one or two more with you, so that BY THE MOUTH OF TWO OR THREE WITNESSES EVERY FACT MAY BE COMFIRMED. And if he refuses to listen to them, tell it to the church; and if he refuses to listen even to the church, let him be to you as a Gentile and a tax-gatherer. (Matthew 18:15-17)

The reference "a Gentile and a tax-gatherer" is to a "heathen or a most despicable person."
G. Campbell Morgan says:

> We must put him outside; we must not allow him to have the shelter of the church; but the moment he is over the borderline, after him, after him, though the way be rough and long, and it means wounding and suffering.[25]

He is emphasizing that there is to be discipline but not "shunning."

It does appear, from Wimber's various trips from Anaheim to Toronto, that the proper scriptural procedure was followed.[26] Let us all understand that "a little leaven leavens the whole lump of dough[.] Clean out the old leaven, that you may be a new lump" (1 Corinthians 5:6-7).

Now let us hope that Vineyard will attempt to follow through on the restoration process that Paul emphasizes in Second Corinthians 2:5-6, 8, 11:

> But if any has caused sorrow . . . [s]ufficient for such a one is this punishment which was inflicted on him by the majority. . . . Wherefore I urge you to reaffirm your love for him . . . in order that

> no advantage be taken of us by Satan;
> for we are not ignorant of his schemes.

There are two vital points that should be noted. First, what I have written clearly shows that there has *not* been a happy severing of relationships, even though John Arnott is quoted as saying, "We will be parting on friendly terms."[27]

Secondly, Marc Dupont prophesied that this great renewal would bring unity to the church.[28] It has not. John Arnott built a revival scheme on this prophecy. Now the very thing prophesied and attempted has resulted in shame to the body of Christ—another split. And the non-Christian and the devil are sitting back and laughing at us all. Please do not mistake it for "holy laughter."

As a minister of long standing, I am frequently asked for opinions on "hot topics." I quite often remark, "You are clever enough to ask that question. I shall be dumb enough to try to answer it." Many people, both laity and clergy, have asked me, "What is your candid opinion of Vineyard, and where do you think it is taking us?"

I have stuck to my original response. And I see no reason to change it now. Vineyard has given a stagnant church a breath of fresh air. However, I believe there are excesses that need to be curbed. If these excesses are not curbed, Vineyard has left itself wide open to heresy. Heresy has a bad habit of creating cults. And cults have a bad habit of becoming "thorn[s] in the flesh" (2 Corinthians

12:7, Numbers 33:55 [in your sides]) of the Church at large.

While in Toronto studying the Toronto Blessing, I had clergy come to my room for interviews. I also went into the "marketplace" to talk to lay people. Already people were jesting about the "animals" in the services. Frequently it was even called the "Animal Church."

I hope and pray that John Arnott and his staff have not started what people, both saved and unsaved, will call the "Animal Cult." It may be too late to stop it, but let us pray that God will intervene.

In a number of books and articles, the writers have declared that we should accept the scriptural process of doing nothing about the situation. This is based on the biblical account of the imprisonment and release of some of the apostles in Acts 5:17-40.

Gamaliel stood before the Council and gave his opinion.

> Men of Israel, take care what you propose to do with these men. . . . [F]or if this plan or action should be of men, it will be overthrown; but if it is of God, you will not be able to overthrow them; or else you may even be found fighting against God. (Acts 5:35, 38-39)

Of course, the Bible is right. This is what happened. But the Bible does not tell us to follow this pattern. In fact the Bible states, "But a certain Pharisee named Gamaliel, a teacher of the Law . . ." (5:34). If we continue to follow Gamaliel's advice, we would have to reject the admonitions of Psalm 1:1—"How blessed is the man who does not walk in the counsel of the wicked, nor stand in the path of sinners, nor sit in the seat of scoffers!"

We should be very careful in examining biblical events to discern whether we are being admonished to follow the example or whether we are being admonished to flee because of the example. If we follow Gamaliel's line of thinking, we would have to conclude that all the cults of our day are of God, because they have not gone away.

From a show of hands in one of the Airport's larger meetings, about half the people indicated they were from overseas. The other half seemed to indicate that they were from either the United States or Canada, but outside the Metropolitan Toronto area. When asked for a show of hands from the Toronto area, less than twenty-five raised their hands.

There has *not* been the great renewal, revival or awakening in Toronto that has "wrapped around the plains of Canada,"[29] as Marc Dupont prophesied, and which John Arnott tried so hard to bring to pass. But I, for one, would have loved to see it happen.

In the meantime, we do know this: On January 20, 1996, the Toronto Airport Vineyard Christian Fellowship publicly announced that it was now the Toronto Airport Christian Fellowship.[30] Vineyard dropped them, and they have dropped the word "Vineyard." How ironic!

When I visited there, the illuminated sign had been changed. The people appeared to me to be very sad. I was able to feel their melancholy when I sat with them. The music pumped them up, but they went right back into their gloom. Experiences had given them a lift, but they had not been grounded in the Word of God, which never changes.

If this book can be used in even a small measure to bring about stability, I will consider it to be of value. I would love to be, once again, a part of another authentic Canadian revival. But I could never categorize the Toronto Blessing as a true renewal, let alone a revival.

> I want to be patient and gentle,
>   Long-suffering and loving and kind,
> As quick to acknowledge my failings
>   As I to another's am blind.
> I want to be quiet and peaceful,
>   Though tempests around me may
>   roll.
> The stillness of Jesus within me,
>   Possessing and filling my soul.[31]

Endnotes

1. Dave Roberts, *The Toronto Blessing* (Eastbourne: Kingsway Publications, 1994), p. 19.

2. Ibid., p. 20.

3. Larry Thomas, *No Laughing Matter* (Excelsior Springs, MO: Double Crown Publishing, 1995), p. 97.

4. Ibid.

5. Marcia Ford in "Toronto Church Ousted from Vineyard," *Charisma*, February 1996, p. 12.

6. Ibid.

7. Ibid., pp. 12-13.

8. *National and International Religion Report*, December 5, 1995 (Vol. 10, No. 1), pp. 4-5.

9. Larry B. Stammer, *The Toronto Star*, Sunday, December 10, 1995, p. A14.

10. Ibid.

11. Ibid.

12. Guy Chevreau, *Catch the Fire* (Toronto, Ontario: Harper-Collins, 1994), p. viii.

13. Doug Koop, "Toronto Airport Vineyard Released to Fly Solo," *Christian Week*, January 2, 1996, pp. 1, 5.

14. *Charisma*, February 1996, p. 12.

15. Mark Parent in an interview with John Arnott, "Testing the Ecclesiology," *Christian Week*, June 20, 1995, p. 7.

16. *Christian Week*, January 2, 1996, p. 5.

17. Ibid.

18. Ibid.

19. Ibid., p. 1.

20. *Charisma*, p. 13.

21. Ibid.

22. Ibid.

23. *National and International Religion Report*, p. 5.

24. *Charisma*, p. 12.

25. G. Campbell Morgan, *The Westminster Pulpit*, Vol. V (London, England: Flemming H. Revell Company, 1954), p. 231.

26. Wimber made at least four trips to the Toronto Airport church over a two year period.

27. *National and International Religion Report*, p. 5.

28. Chevreau, p. 29.

29. See Marc Dupont's prophecy as recorded on p. 27.

30. Sue Careless, *Christian Week*, February 13, 1996, p. 1.

31. A.B. Simpson, "I Want to Be Holy," *Hymns of the Christian Life* (Camp Hill, PA: Christian Publications, 1978), #235.

Epilogue

My good friend William McAlpine, a professor at Canadian Bible College/Theological Seminary in Regina, Saskatchewan, directs a one-year Bible-college course called "Access." It is designed to assist students to gain access to the world at large, giving them a viable overall view of the Word of God, intermingled with practical experience.

Each year students participate in what is called "InterSession." This calls for the students to be trained in a completely different cultural situation in various parts of the nation. One such group goes into northern Saskatchewan with workers experienced in wilderness activities.

In a day of "doing one's own thing," there is a strong tendency for people to ignore what has been proven to be successful and safe and is perhaps the only way there is to correctly do certain things. Unfortunately there are times when our personal intuitions, interpretations or opinions may be very misleading.

For example, to navigate through the great forests, a person must have two vital things—a reliable compass and a firm resolution to follow the directives of that compass.

In this program, students are given a good compass and a flashlight and sent into the woods at night in pairs. They have their instructions. They are given a certain bearing and told to walk straight ahead for 150 paces. Then they must take a bearing ninety degrees to the right and take 100 paces in that direction. This is to be repeated, ninety degrees to the right for another 100 paces. And again, it is to be done once more.

The last thing the students are told before they go into the rather dense bush is this: "Believe your compass!"

Now if they pace accurately, read their compass correctly and *believe* their compass, they should intersect their original path, fifty paces from their point of entry and easily be able to return to the starting point.

Every year at least two pairs of students "mess up" because they do not believe their compass. They go with their inner feelings or a misinterpretation of the lay of the land. This gives an excellent illustration for both the lost ones and all the rest. It is critical for everyone to obey the compass. Circumstances may be yelling, "This way! This way!" Our intuitions may be responding, "No! This way!" When each in the set of two are at odds in the matter, generally the more forceful one gets the nod. Often this results in being lost in the forest.

McAlpine says:

To ignore one's compass in the bush

can ultimately lead to unnecessary challenges, and even death itself, given the right combination of circumstances. Similarly, failure to follow our spiritual compass, the Word of God, can likewise lead to challenges altogether unnecessary.[1]

What a powerful message this is! We have the Word of God. It is our compass. It is the *only* accurate spiritual compass we have, and it is completely unbiased. It does not bend according to our whims and desires; it does not change from day to day.

Our personalities can never change God's Word, but God's Word can change our personalities. Our beliefs cannot change the Bible, but the Bible can change our beliefs. Properly read and obeyed, it will keep us forever from going astray. After all, it is God's Word! It was written at the command of God and speaks to us by the voice of His Holy Spirit.

What does the Holy Spirit say about the Toronto Blessing? Exactly what the Word says, and that is what I have attempted to present in the pages of this book. Looking for the easy route and neglecting the Word of God in order to follow other agendas often leads to heartache, turmoil and even destruction. This is not to discount the gift of prophecy as long as it does not contradict the teachings of Scripture.

The Bible says to "pray without ceasing" (1

Thessalonians 5:17). It is time to get off our backs on the floor and get down on our knees in humility before God, seek His face and turn from our wicked ways. *Then* He will hear from heaven, forgive our sin and heal our land (2 Chronicles 7:14).

Always remember your compass!

> As of old He walked t' Emmaus,
>   With them to abide;
> So, through all life's way He walketh,
>   Ever near our side.
> Soon again we shall behold Him—
>   Hasten, Lord, the day!
> But 'twill still be this same Jesus,
>   As He went away.[2]

Endnotes

1. William McAlpine, InterSession, Regina, Saskatchewan, unpublished notes, February 1996.

2. A.B. Simpson, "Yesterday, Today, Forever," *Hymns of the Christian Life* (Camp Hill, PA: Christian Publications, 1978), #119.

Bibliography

Arnott, John. *The Father's Blessing*. Lake Mary, FL: Creation House, 1995.

Barron, Bruce. *The Health and Wealth Gospel*. Downers Grove, IL: InterVarsity, 1987.

Beverley, James A. *Holy Laughter and the Toronto Blessing*. Grand Rapids, MI: Zondervan, 1995.

Buckingham, Jamie. *Daughter of Destiny*. Plainsfield, NJ: Logos International, 1976.

Burgess, Stanley M., and McGee, Gary B., eds. *The Dictionary of Pentecostal and Charismatic Movements*. Grand Rapids, MI: Zondervan, 1988.

Calvin, John. *Calvin's Commentary*. Grand Rapids, MI: Baker Book House, reprinted 1984.

Campbell, Duncan. *The Price and Power of Revival*. Edinburgh, Scotland: Faith Mission, n.d.

Cannon, Stephen F. *Benny Hinn and Revelation Knowledge*. St. Louis, MO: Personal Freedom Outreach, 1995.

Chambers, J. Oswald. *Heresies and Cults*. London: Lakeland, 1971.

Chevreau, Guy. *Catch the Fire*. London, ON: Harper-Collins, 1994.

Cross, Edward. *Miracles, Demons, and Spiritual Warfare*. Grand Rapids, MI: Baker Book House, n.d.

De Arteaga, William. *Quenching the Spirit*. Altamonte, FL: Creation House, 1992.

Dickson, David. *A Commentary on the Psalms*. Minneapolis, MN: Klock and Klock Christian Publications, 1980.

Dixon, Patrick. *Signs of Revival*. Eastbourne, England: Kingsway, 1994.

Edwards, Jonathan. *On Revival*. Edinburgh, Scotland: Banner of Truth, 1991.

————. *The Works of Jonathan Edwards*. Edinburgh, Scotland: Banner of Truth, 1992.

Enns, Paul P. *Bible Study Commentary*. Grand Rapids, MI: Zondervan, 1982.

Finney, Charles G. *Lectures on Revival*. Minneapolis, MN: Bethany House, 1988.

Fisher, G. Richard, and Goedelman, M. Kurt. *The Confusing Word of Benny Hinn*. St. Louis, MO: Personal Freedom Outreach, 1995.

Foster, K. Neill. *The Third View of Tongues*. Camp Hill, PA: Christian Publications, 1994.

Graham, Billy. *The Holy Spirit*. Waco, TX: Word, 1978.

Gray and Adams Bible Commentary. Grand Rapids, MI: Zondervan, n.d.

Gunstone, John. *Signs and Wonders: The Wimber Phenomenon*. London: Daybreak 1989.

Hanegraaff, Hank. *Christianity in Crisis*. Eugene, OR: Harvest House, 1993.

Hillstrom, Elizabeth L. *Testing the Spirits*. Downers Grove, IL: InterVarsity, 1995.

Hinn, Benny. *The Anointing*. Nashville, TN: Thomas Nelson, 1992.

_____. *Good Morning, Holy Spirit.* Nashville, TN: Thomas Nelson, 1990.

Horton, Michael. *Agony of Deceit.* Chicago: Moody, 1990.

Howard-Browne, Rodney. *The Touch of God.* Louisville, KY: Rodney Howard-Browne Evangelistic Assn., Inc., 1992.

Hymns of the Christian Life. Camp Hill, PA: Christian Publications, Inc., 1978.

Kenyon, Essek W. *New Creation Realities.* Lynwood, WA: Kenyon's Gospel Publishing Society, 1945.

Kuglin, Robert J. *Handbook on the Holy Spirit.* Camp Hill, PA: Christian Publications, 1996.

Kuhlman, Kathryn. *I Believe in Miracles.* New York: Pyramid Books, 1969.

Lundy, Daniel G. *Signs and Wonders.* Richmond Hill, ON: Canadian Christian Publications, 1992.

Lutzer, Erwin W. *Flames of Freedom.* Chicago: Moody Press, 1976.

MacArthur, John F., Jr. *Charismatic Chaos.* Grand Rapids, MI: Zondervan, 1992.

McIntosh, C.H. *Notes on Exodus.* New York: Loizeaux Brothers, n.d.

McLelland, Frank, and Oatley-Willis, Bert. *The Toronto Blessing: Christian Faith or Charismatic Feeling.* Toronto: Wittenburg Publications, 1995.

Neale, J.M. and Littledale, R.F. *A Commentary on the Psalms.* New York: AMS Press Company, 1976.

Nolen, William A. Healing: *A Doctor in Search of a Miracle.* Greenwich, CT: Fawcett Publications, 1974.

Rawlyk, George A. *The Canada Fire: Radical Evangelicalism in British North America, 1775-1812*. Montreal: McGill-Queen's University Press, 1944.

Riss, Richard. *The Latter Rain Movement of 1948 and Mid-twentieth Century Awakening*. Vancouver, BC: Regent College, 1979.

_____. *A Survey of 20th Century Revival Movements in North America*. Peabody, MA: Hendrickson, Pubs., Inc., 1988.

Roberts, Dave. *The Toronto Blessing*. Eastbourne, England: Kingsway Publications, 1994.

Rosell, Garth M. and Dupuis, Richard A.G., eds. *The Memoirs of Charles G. Finney: The Complete Restored Text*. Grand Rapids, MI: Zondervan, 1989.

Simpson, A.B. *The Gospel of Healing*. Camp Hill, PA: Christian Publications, 1982.

Smith, John E., ed. *Jonathan Edwards, Religious Affections*. New Haven, CT: Yale University Press, 1969.

Smith, William. *A Dictonary of the Bible*. Chicago: Fleming H. Revell Co., n.d.

Snyder, Howard. *Signs of the Spirit*. Grand Rapids, MI: Zondervan, 1989.

Snyder, James L. *In Pursuit of God: The Life of A.W. Tozer*. Camp Hill, PA: Christian Publications, 1991.

Tari, Mel. *Like a Mighty Wind*. Carol Stream, IL: Creation House, 1972.

Thomas, Larry. *No Laughing Matter*. Excelsior Springs, MO: Double Crown,1995.

Tozer, A.W. *I Call it Heresy*. Camp Hill, PA: Christian Publications, 1974.

_____. *God Tells the Man Who Cares*. Camp Hill, PA: Christian Publications, 1970.

_____. *I Talk Back to the Devil*. Camp Hill, PA: Christian Publication, 1972.

Warfield, Benjamin, B. *Counterfeit Miracles*. Carlisle, PA: Banner of Truth, 1918.

Weaver, C. Douglas. *The Healer Prophet, William Marrion Branham*. Macon, GA: Mercer University Press, 1987.

Whittacker, Colin. *Great Revivals*. London: Marshall Pickering, 1990.

Whyte, H.A. Maxwell. *The Power of the Blood*. Springdale, PA: Whitaker House, 1973.

Wimber, John, and Springer, Kevin. *Power Evangelism*. San Francisco: Harper & Row, 1986.

_____. *Power Healing*. San Francisco: Harper & Row, 1987

The World Book Encyclopedia. Chicago: Field Enterprises Educational Corporation, 1973.

Young, Robert. *Young's Analytical Concordance to the Bible*. New York: Funk and Wagnalls, n.d.